Thirsting for God

C000079819

Thirsting for God

ROBERT LLEWELYN

DARTON·LONGMAN+TODD

First published in 2000 by
Darton, Longman and Todd Ltd
1 Spencer Court
140–142 Wandsworth High Street
London SW18 4JJ

ISBN 0–232–52365–7

A catalogue record for this book is available from the British Library.

*All royalties earned by the sale of this book are being given to the
Community of the Sisters of the Love of God of the Convent of
the Incarnation, Fairacres, Oxford.*

Designed by Sandie Boccacci
Phototypeset in 9.5/11.5pt Palatino by Intype London Ltd
Printed and bound in Great Britain by
Page Bros, Norwich, Norfolk

Contents

Foreword

In the past twenty years, through his connection with the Julian Shrine, and through his many writings, Robert Llewelyn has become known as one of the most respected and trusted spiritual teachers in the Church. These homilies date from the years immediately before he went to Norwich. They show the capacities and formation which he brought with him to the work of the last twenty years. His words have an extraordinary clarity about them like fresh, running water. They are sometimes deceptively simple; they do not always yield up their true value at first reading. They challenge the reader not only to new ways of action but to new ways of thinking.

These pages come from a mind which is well stored with material both from scripture and tradition, a mind which at times overflows with wisdom. They are the product of a life in which prayer and action, reflection and practical concern have come together in a remarkable and eloquent unity. Outwardly unadorned, they prove unexpectedly nourishing for the life within.

A.M. ALLCHIN

Preface

From 1972 to 1975 I was warden at Bede House near Staplehurst in Kent. This is a foundation of the Sisters of the Love of God, whose Mother House is at Fairacres in Oxford. Bede House was founded in 1966 by Mother Mary Clare of Fairacres in conjunction with its (Fairacres) warden, Father Gilbert Shaw. It is an idyllic place, set in the heart of the Kent countryside. Its chapel is the ground floor of a picturesque redundant oast house. Above is a well-stocked library devoted to books in the great spiritual tradition. Its former farmhouse, with its ancient, if threatening-looking, timbers accommodates three or four working (cenobitic) sisters, whilst in the wooden Colt houses scattered throughout the grounds two or three hermits live or test out their vocation. Their life is devoted to prayer, silence and gardening or some other useful work. This leaves room, again in Colt houses, for several guests. The cenobitic sisters sang their daily offices together in the chapel, and their night office at two o'clock each morning. There is a daily eucharist which the hermits might or might not attend according to their rule. All would be present on Sundays.

Such was the congregation each Sunday morning to whom I would deliver these and other homilies. They are coloured some-what by the make-up of the small congregation, the few visitors being, perhaps, clergy in need of a quiet weekend or religious or others well instructed in the faith. I have put together, in a form suitable for reading, a selection of the addresses which have survived. The homilies have generally been shortened, and where I have thought it would be helpful, brief development or clarifi-cation has been made. It will be understood that with such a specialised congregation I could take for granted a background of scriptural and theological knowledge beyond what one would expect to find in a parish church. It is hoped that these homilies may make acceptable meditational material for a wider audience. They are intended to be given space and taken one at a time. To read the book in a few sittings would be likely to give spiritual indigestion.

Scriptural texts quoted in the homilies were taken from the translation judged to suit the context best and so remain unchanged in bringing the addresses to print. Where the gospel or other passage is set out at the beginning of a homily it has for copyright reasons been taken from the New Jerusalem Bible. Scriptural passages – in a number of cases shortened – are set out only where the homily has bearing on the passage as a whole. In other cases the scriptural reference is given to enable the reader to refer to the passage if desired.

I dedicate this book gratefully to the Sisters of the Love of God who encouraged me by their love and prayers, and I offer it as a thanksgiving to God for blessings over many years.

ROBERT LLEWELYN

Heroic Love

The greatest commandment of all

One of the scribes who had listened to them debating appreciated
that Jesus had given a good answer and put a further question to
him, 'Which is the first of all the commandments?' Jesus replied,
'This is the first: Listen, Israel, the Lord our God is the one, only
Lord, and you must love the Lord your God with all your heart,
with all your soul, with all your mind and with all your strength.
The second is this: You must love your neighbour as yourself. There
is no commandment greater than these.' The scribe said to him, 'Well
spoken, Master; what you have said is true, that he is one and
there is no other. To love him with all your heart, with all your
understanding and strength, and to love your neighbour as yourself,
this is far more important than any burnt offering or sacrifice.' Jesus,
seeing how wisely he had spoken, said, 'You are not far from the
kingdom of God.' And after that no one dared to question him any
more. (Mark 12:28–34)

'You shall love[1] the Lord your God with all your heart, and
with all your mind, and with all your soul, and with all
your strength, and your neighbour as yourself.'

I have recently been reading of a concentration camp experience under the title of 'Only love is necessary'. Petra, the
writer, tells how in a certain camp he met Father Onaphrius, a
monk of Mount Athos who had been sentenced to twenty years'
imprisonment for sheltering a wanted person in his monastery.
He finds Father Onaphrius praying and later he asks him if he
prays for the communist guards as well as the inmates. 'Of
course I do,' he is told, 'for they too are God's children.' This
evidently made a great impression on Petra for later he writes,
'I strove with all my strength to love and to love all men equally
without exception or omission'.

Then came the testing. Petra's companion, an elderly man of

1

seventy, was savagely beaten up by the commandant for resting during a work period. Petra bent himself across the old man's body to protect him from further blows. It was too late, for the older man died without regaining consciousness. After Petra himself had taken several blows from a spade on head and body, the guards were called and he was put in a freezingly cold cell the shape of a sentry box, so small that it was impossible even to sit down. 'To pray in such circumstances,' he wrote, 'is not easy but it is a great and sweet solace if one can do so, and one must try with all one's strength to love more and not less. I had to struggle not to sink below the level of love, to love Luca the commandant, not for a moment but continuously. I had to drive my soul to do this as one may push a car with locked brakes.' And then he adds this revealing comment, that when it came to loving his friends he found it natural and easy and he loved them more deeply than before.

It is, we may believe, of God's mercy that we are spared Petra's test for in such circumstances we might find ourselves utterly defeated. But the times of the testing of our love come in one way or another to us all and we ought to be grateful and not grudging, as we sometimes are, when the trial presented to us is severe. 'I had to drive my soul,' says Petra, in a powerful figure of speech, 'as one may push a car with locked brakes.' I suppose that if one makes a habit of pushing cars with the brakes on one builds up a reserve of physique which makes it fairly easy to push those which run freely. This at least was his experience and we may believe that it is only when our love is tried and tested in the place where we are most vulnerable that we can ever really be established in love in the ordinary relationships of life. Yet, how easily do we shrink from such testing experiences, or complain of them secretly in our hearts, or perhaps not so secretly, unmindful of the weight of glory which this experience, accepted in faith as coming within the providential ordering of our lives, may work within us and through us to those around.

Yet, how is it we are to obey our Lord's command that we shall love completely with heart and mind and soul? We know that it is beyond us now and we can only pray that we may grow. Once we have done that we already have the beginnings of what we pray for. Where love is still beyond our reach it can be a help to say: 'Lord, you know I am unable to love this person, but I know that you love them wholly and completely. For the present I am content to rest in that.'

Our collect reminds us that love does not find its source in ourselves: 'Send thy Holy Spirit and pour into our hearts that most excellent gift of love.' For St John of the Cross this most excellent gift is the fruit of contemplation and it is this aspect which has special relevance to all who are moving on in the Christian life. John describes contemplation as a peaceful and loving inflow of God which inflames the soul with the spirit of love.[2] As a child's love is evoked by the love of its parents so is our love drawn out by the inflow of the love of God. All that is asked of us is that we quietly and relaxedly allow God time and space, being careful at the same time not to hinder his designs by a misguided eagerness to receive him. The one who floats has to lie back and trust themself unreservedly to the water, at the same time making almost unperceived adjustments to the ripples or waves. So will it be in contemplation, a gentle correspondence – impatience or restlessness would spoil everything – with God's action upon us.

'Multiply love in us, O Father of love, that we may please thee well, serve thee best, glorify thee most, who has first loved us.'[3] Amen.

1. Greek: *agape*; for fuller meaning see chapter 27.
2. See Book 1 of *The Dark Night of the Soul*, 10:6.
3. *My God and my Glory*, ed. Eric Milner-White (SPCK, 1954).

∼2∼

The Dangers of Judging

Do not Judge

'Do not judge, and you will not be judged; because the judgements
you give are the judgements you will get, and the standard you use
will be the standard used for you. Why do you observe the splinter
in your brother's eye and never notice the great log in your own?
And how dare you say to your brother, "Let me take that splinter
out of your eye," when, look, there is a great log in your own?
Hypocrite! Take the log out of your own eye first, and then you will
see clearly enough to take the splinter out of your brother's eye.'

(Matthew 7:1–5)

'Judge not that you may not be judged' is an arresting phrase
from today's gospel (Matthew 7:1–12). And that, no doubt, is
what it is intended to be – arresting – using the word in its basic
sense of stopping a person in their tracks, bidding us to pause
and take a brief look at ourselves and see how far we deviate or
conform.

It was the method of Jesus to make his teaching vivid by using
the language of metaphor or proverb. In this very sermon on the
mount from which this teaching comes we are bidden in certain
circumstances to pluck out the eye or cut off the foot or the hand
which offends, and these are striking and vigorous figures of
speech. Later we have a series of sayings of the nature of prov-
erbs, such as 'If a man strikes you on one cheek you are to turn
to him the other'. A proverb might be defined as a short, easily
remembered saying embodying a principle but not laying down
a rule applicable to all occasions. The principle here is that
Christian love is to be so absolute, so demanding upon a person's
character, that no limit can be placed on its manifestation, even
to turning again to one's aggressor to be struck a second time.
But the application of that principle will vary. Salvationist
preachers of former days, in the face of hostile gatherings, must

4

often have obeyed in an almost literal sense. Yet when next day, as would probably have been true in a few cases, the preacher returned to his profession as a policeman, a different response would have been proper even though the universal principle of love remained.

So, too, the words of Jesus that we are not to judge embody an important principle but they do not lay down a universal rule. There are examples of Jesus himself judging. He judged Peter as playing the role of Satan when he tried to deflect him from his Passion, he judged Herod as 'that fox', he judged the Pharisees for their arrogance and blindness. Lest it be argued that he alone might be exempted from this precept, we may recall how we, too, are bidden to 'judge righteous judgements' (John 7:24). Furthermore, it is widely assumed that in the confessional there belongs to the priest the function of judging in the 'binding and loosing' of penitents, based on the post-resurrection words of Jesus (John 20:23).

The words of Jesus quoted in our text warning us against judgement of others must be understood partly through the context in which they are placed. They are followed immediately by the parable of the mote and the beam. No person may judge another until he has first judged himself, or better, using the imagery of St John, until he has first allowed the Holy Spirit of righteousness and truth, to search out the secret places of the heart, and purge him of his own guilt and sin. Once we have submitted ourselves to the surgery of the Holy Spirit it is certain that we shall have little mind to judge others, and such judgements which our position in society may call upon us to make, will be exercised in a spirit of meekness, understanding and love. Moreover, it is only such a one whose judgements will be objective, who will, in the words of Jesus, judge righteous judgement, that is to say judge in accordance with the truth. Those who have not passed through the testing fires of the Spirit will be likely to judge not only contemptuously but superficially. As likely as not we shall then project our own undiscovered faults on to those whom we judge. Moreover we shall be in danger of seeing in others the sins we would like to have committed ourselves, if we had had the courage or the opportunity. Lastly, our judgements will in such cases be likely to be vain, serving no useful purpose in helping the other, for they will have proceeded from an inferior motive such as bitterness or jealousy or wounded pride.

Finally, none of us can pronounce a final judgement upon another. That is a prerogative which belongs to God alone for it is only to him that all hearts are open and all desires known. We can never probe the secrets of another's heart, we can never be aware of the force of the temptations or of the psychological twists in another person's nature. Nor can we ever know of the fears which may beset another or of the fires of passion which may burn within. Nor again can we know the prayers of the heart or the cries for deliverance which may stamp and colour the secret stretches of another's life. But there is yet more, and this should be an occasion for hope. Not only can we not judge another; we cannot, as St Paul tells us, even judge ourselves (1 Corinthians 4:3). If we attempt to do so, it is likely to be that our judgement will fall far short of God's merciful and omniscient judgement. It will be a mark of every growing Christian to turn away from preoccupation with self-judgement which often exerts a secret fascination, concealing within itself a disguised desire for self-justification. We are to turn from this to an ever-deepening and constantly renewed confidence in God, committing ourselves, in the words of Peter, into the hands of him who judges righteously.

～3～

Salt, Light, Perfection

Salt for the earth and light for the world

'You are salt for the earth. But if salt loses its taste, what can make it salty again? It is good for nothing, and can only be thrown out to be trampled under people's feet.

'You are light for the world. A city built on a hill-top cannot be hidden. No one lights a lamp to put it under a tub; they put it on the lamp-stand where it shines for everyone in the house. In the same way your light must shine in people's sight, so that, seeing your good works, they may give praise to your Father in heaven.'

(Matthew 5:13–16)

I take words from our gospel (Matthew 5:13–20): 'You are the salt of the earth'. The obvious thing to say about salt is that it flavours and this seems to be the primary thought of Jesus in using this figure of speech, for he at once goes on to ask of what use is salt if it loses its power to season our food. Salt brings out the taste of food in a manner quite disproportionate to the quantity used. As salt makes evident to the palate the true quality of food, so Christians are to be a savouring influence in society, bringing out what is best in others, enabling them to be as God intended. I suppose we have all known people who have seemed to have some strange magic in enabling us to be fuller, more complete, more liberated and spontaneous than we often know ourselves to be. And it is our hope that others may have experienced this in relation to ourselves, almost certainly chiefly when we are least conscious of it. The saints are those who have this quality in a peculiar degree. People used to remark in the life of Bishop King of the past century how he would walk through the old-fashioned fairgrounds of Lincoln with their merry-go-rounds and hoop-la stalls and sideshows, and draw out from simple and rough-living people gentleness and affection and warmth simply by his presence among them.

7

The supreme manifestation of this radiance must have been in the life of our Lord himself, the life which was the light of all, full of grace and truth. It is this light which is to shine within us and through us as Jesus tells us in this same gospel passage: 'You are the light of the world and you are to let your light so shine among others that your works may be known and your father glorified.' This transformation, as we know so well, takes place within us as we grow more fully into Christ, into the power of his resurrection life, a work which goes on without ceasing in those whose wills are held in him, unceasingly whether in work or conversation or sleep or suffering or eucharist or prayer. Every breath we take may be a bringing to completion the good work the Spirit has begun in us in baptism.

God's plan for us is nothing short of perfection. 'You must be perfect (or complete) as your heavenly Father is perfect' (Matthew 5:48). And that is for all of us, whether for priests or religious, parents or children, company directors or shop stewards, privileged or deprived. But it is we who are to be perfect and not our works, though our works will always bear a close relationship to what we are.

Perfectionism – the deliberate seeking of perfection – can be fraught with moral danger and it is safer when we understand the concept adverbially rather than adjectivally; which remark no doubt needs elucidation. Looking back to Jesus the carpenter I suggest that he made tables 'perfectly', perfectly being an adverb and referring to the manner of making. But I do not suppose that he always made perfect tables, perfect being an adjective and referring to the quality of the finished product. There may have been occasions when seasoned wood was not available, or the tools were inadequate, or the pressure of work did not allow him to put into this or that door or table or plough the time he would have wished to give. Yet the word perfection applied, not because the finished product was technically speaking perfect, but because it issued from a life perfectly offered in love and obedience to the Father, and implicit in that would be the complete dedication of talents given and skills achieved. It is in this sense that Christian perfection will manifest itself and to say that is not, of course, to excuse second-rate performance when the situation allows for something better.

The woman who put a farthing into the temple alms box can

hardly have made a perfect offering from the point of view of the treasurer of the temple, yet Jesus, being aware of all the circumstances, commended her for the perfection of love which the gift disclosed. And so we try to bring all our love to what we do (for therein lies true perfection) without worrying ourselves crazy about the end product of our work. 'Good works are the most perfect,' St John of the Cross reminds us, 'when they are wrought in the most pure and sincere love of God, and with the least regard to our own present and future interests, or to joy and sweetness, consolation and praise.' Little deeds motivated by love become great deeds in God's sight. An expression of love, however small it may seem in the eyes of the giver, is never wasted and may be used by God for the enrichment of his kingdom beyond anything we could guess or imagine.

~4~

Prayer Defeating Evil

The Baptist's question. Jesus commends him

Now John had heard in prison what Christ was doing and he sent his disciples to ask him. 'Are you the one who is to come, or are we to expect someone else?' Jesus answered, 'Go back and tell John what you hear and see; the blind see again, and the lame walk, those suffering from virulent skin-diseases are cleansed, and the deaf hear, the dead are raised to life and the good news is proclaimed to the poor; and blessed is anyone who does not find me a cause of falling.'

(Matthew 11:2–6)

The gospel reading (Matthew 11:1–15) tells of St John the Baptist languishing in the dungeons of Herod Antipas. It may not be the right interpretation of the passage but it seems to be the more natural one, that St John's own faith was being severely tried (there are those who say it was his disciples and not himself who were being tested), and that he sent his disciples to Jesus in the hope of finding personal reassurance in the message they would bring back. Jesus tells them that they are to speak to John of what is taking place, the blind receiving their sight, the lame being healed, the lepers being made clean, the deaf being made to hear, and the poor having the gospel preached to them. There follows a eulogy of John proclaiming him as the greatest of the old order, and yet (in privilege) less than the least of those called to the new.

As we think of St John, lonely and dejected and perhaps ill-treated in his prison fortress, our thoughts will naturally go to the many people of our day – and not only of our day – who are suffering imprisonment or deprivation for their witness to the truth. At the present time it seems that some, through the protests of the media or private organisations, are able to increase slightly their prospect of just treatment; yet for every two or three who catch the public eye, there are, as we know, thousands who have no one of influence to plead their cause.

It was, so far as I know, coincidental, and nothing to do with our gospel story, that I turned again this week to Richard Wurmbrandt's *Sermons in Solitary Confinement*. For three years Pastor Wurmbrandt lived alone in an underground cell in a Romanian prison, the silence broken only by the days of fearful interrogation by the Secret Police. It is, we are told, a marvel of medical history that he is alive to tell the story. Night after night he composed sermons preached to himself, the only way open to the preservation of his faith and sanity.

In one of the three chapters which I read again he tells of a spider in his cell, his sole companion whom he loved and tended and fed. The little creature, so it seemed to him, became agitated and excited the day before a new bout of terror burst upon him and other prisoners. And he tells how in other imprisonments when he had a cell above ground, and could look through the window into the prison yard, the pigeons would give advance warning of terrors to come by the agitated flapping of their wings; and how other prisoners had given him further examples of psychic awareness from the animal world. No doubt we have met the same phenomenon in human beings, who sometimes pick up beforehand the knowledge of some disaster or terror. Some terrible wickedness is being planned and perhaps gloated over by the powers of evil. We are up against depravity and evil on a cosmic scale, what St Paul calls principalities and powers and spiritual wickedness in high places, which it is the work of every person of prayer to resist. This is, in a special way, our work in a community such as this. 'Men of action' it has been said 'are up against symptoms; whereas contemplatives war against the causes which lie behind the symptoms.'

It was at this point in my reading that the well-known words of *The Cloud of Unknowing* came to my mind. 'It is the work' (referring to the author's own way of contemplative prayer) 'which pleases God most. All the saints and angels of God rejoice over it, and hasten to help it on with all their might. All the demons, however, are furious at what you are doing and try to defeat it in every conceivable way. Yes, the very souls in purgatory find their prayer eased by virtue of your work.'

The nurse who takes nourishment or medicine to her patient can see then and there, or at least shortly afterwards, what is achieved through her ministrations. And being thus encouraged

11

it may not be difficult for her to go on. In prayer we cannot see in any comparable way, we have only the perception of faith. If only we could see that when we are faithful in prayer there is a pushing back of the walls of evil by the forces of good, a breaking up of the kingdom of darkness by a penetration of light, a dispelling of the mists of error by the power of truth, what encouragement there would be! Just occasionally the veil is lifted and we (perhaps through the witness of others) are made aware, but for the most part it is a matter of being constant and going on in the power of faith. We need to affirm to ourselves, and to one another, that all humankind is affected by the prayers of the faithful; and too, if we may believe the *Cloud*, (for their gladness) the angels; and (for their confusion) the powers of darkness; and yes, (after their manner) the pigeons and even the spider which, in its littleness and poverty, ministered to a suffering man.

5

Christianity and Other Faiths

'The true light that enlightens every man was coming into the world' (John 1:9). St John wrote 'every man', not 'every Christian', but everybody. Commenting on this text Archbishop Temple wrote:

> All that is noble in non-Christian conduct or thought or worship is the work of Christ upon them and within them. By the word of God – that is to say, by Jesus Christ – Isaiah and Plato and Zoroaster and Buddha and Confucius conceived and uttered such truths as they declared. There is only one divine light and every man in his measure is enlightened by it.[1]

St Paul has a similar thought with regard to the Jews, when looking back to the days of Moses in the wilderness. He writes: 'they drank of the spiritual rock which followed them, and that rock was Christ' (1 Corinthians 10:4). And from the lips of Jesus we have: 'Before Abraham was, I am' (John 8:58).

I would like to reflect on what we may call the universal Christ or the cosmic Christ, the Christ who may be deeply at work in 'every man coming into the world' without that man or woman being aware that this is so. The paradox is that some who know him most may know him least, and that others who seem not to know him at all may know him best of all. We have it from Jesus himself that many that are first shall be last and many that are last shall be first.

I think of two groups of people. The first consists of the relatives of Jesus who came to see him during his ministry when he was preaching and healing the sick. These men and women knew Jesus well, in many ways better than we can ever know him. They had been brought up with him, they were familiar with his appearance, his voice, his gestures, his habits, his conversation in the home, his work as a carpenter, his love of nature, and so on. And yet in spite of all their knowledge, in the only way that really mattered, they didn't know him at all. They tried to take him home, to force him to desist from his work; they said, 'You are mad, you are beside yourself' (Mark 3:21).

There is the one group. And the second one, too, comes from the Bible. It is those of whom Jesus spoke in what we know as the parable of the sheep and the goats (Matthew 25:31–46). To those on his right hand he says: 'I was hungry and you fed me, thirsty and you gave me drink, naked and you clothed me, sick and in prison and you visited me.' They protested that they had never even met him. How could they have done such things? 'Truly, I say that inasmuch as you did it to the least of these my brethren you did it unto me.' These men and women, they did not know Jesus at all. And yet in the only way that ultimately mattered they knew him best of all.

What happened in former days when missionaries went out from this land to take Christ to those of other faiths? We knew Christ – or at least we thought we did – we had the record of the scriptures, the theological training, and it is to be hoped that we bore him in our hearts. If that is so we were well equipped. But too often we forgot that, although we took him, he was there before us, and although we had a treasure to give out of the rich heritage which was ours, we had, too, much to receive from other traditions. The witness in the heart may well have been deeper in some we went to teach than in ourselves.

I have in mind today two people I met in India. One was the Hindu doctor of a large leper hospital founded at Wardha in Central India by Mahatma Gandhi. This man showed me round his hospital. The patients were, many of them, in a pitiable condition. My doctor friend was so obviously happy in his work, a work poorly rewarded in material terms, but for him rich in friendship and in opportunity for serving these very poor, suffering and underprivileged people. I could not imagine him leaving the work for a well-paid practice in Delhi or Bombay.

That was one man, and the second I met in the guest room of a Hindu ashram nearby. An ashram, as I expect you know, is a community something like a monastery or convent, only on more simple and less structured lines. One doesn't get a room to oneself. I think there were about eight of us in the guest room and three beds, five sleeping on the floor. At the foot of my bed, eating his breakfast when I awoke in the morning was Brother Ramananda, as I shall call him, for I cannot remember his real name. Brother Ramananda was a Hindu who owned nothing except his clothes and a blanket, portions of the scriptures and a few kitchen utensils. Every day he would walk to one or another of thirty villages within a radius of fifteen miles to gather round him Hindu children and teach them to pray. In return, grateful parents would supply him with his one substantial meal of the day. One day he told me he was going to a certain village where Elizabeth lived, the only Christian child amongst the many to whom he ministered. Did I, by any chance, have something he could take her, a picture or a cross or a prayer card, as he would like her to have something from her own religion? I happened to have a card with the picture of a crucifix which I gladly passed on, and later he told me how pleased Elizabeth had been to receive it. I can't describe Brother Ramananda adequately, his happiness and his simple trust in God to supply his needs, but I thought of him as one of the early Franciscan brothers and as one of God's saints.

There is a much-loved story in the Bible (Luke 24:13–35) which I often think of as an enacted parable. Two people were on the road from Jerusalem to Emmaus when they were joined by a stranger who talked with them in the way. They did not know who he was until evening time when his identity became clear in the breaking of the bread. For Brother Ramananda and the leprosy doctor and many like them, the eventide of life has not yet come. But come it must, and the stranger will reveal himself and they will say: 'Did not our heart burn within us as we walked with him in the way?' They will discover that they had known Christ all the time without knowing that they knew him.

I close with a story which was told to some of us by Dr Stanley Jones, an American Methodist missionary who had worked many years in India. Dr Stanley Jones, as often happened, was speaking of Christ to a mixed group of Christians and Hindus and others in Bombay. After his talk an elderly and devout Hindu came to the platform and said, 'Sir, I thank you, I have known him all my life and now you have told me his name'.

It is a great blessing that his name may be known amongst all peoples, though it is as nothing if his presence is not carried in our hearts.

1. *Readings in St John's Gospel*, William Temple (Macmillan, 1939).

~6~

The Place of Petitionary Prayer

The Lord's prayer

Now it happened that he was in a certain place praying, and when he had finished one of his disciples said, 'Lord, teach us to pray, as John taught his disciples.' He said to them, 'When you pray, this is what to say:

> Father, may your name be held holy,
> your kingdom come;
> give us each day our daily bread,
> and forgive us our sins,
> for we ourselves forgive each one who is in debt to us.
> And do not put us to the test.'

The importunate friend

He also said to them, 'Suppose one of you has a friend and goes to him in the middle of the night to say, "My friend, lend me three loaves, because a friend of mine on his travels has just arrived at my house and I have nothing to offer him;" and the man answers from inside the house, "Do not bother me. The door is bolted now, and my children are with me in bed; I cannot get up to give it to you." I tell you, if the man does not get up and give it him for friendship's sake, persistence will make him get up and give his friend all he wants.

Effective prayer

'So I say to you: Ask, and it will be given to you; search, and you will find; knock, and the door will be opened to you. For everyone who asks receives; everyone who searches finds; everyone who knocks will have the door opened. What father among you, if his son asked for a fish, would hand him a snake? Or if he asked for an egg, hand him a scorpion? If you then, evil as you are, know how to give your children what is good, how much more will the heavenly Father give the Holy Spirit to those who ask him!' (Luke 11:1–13)

Our gospel reading is given up entirely to the teaching of Jesus on prayer. When the word 'prayer' is used in the Bible it always refers to petitionary prayer. Of course we know the Bible is rich in praise, adoration, thanksgiving, confession of sin, colloquy with God as well as petition. But of these varied aspects of worship it is only petition which is called prayer.[1]

Our gospel is no exception to the general rule. Throughout its thirteen verses it is petitionary prayer of which Jesus speaks. First we have the Lord's Prayer itself with its six petitonary clauses, then the parable of the householder, which encourages perseverance. The verses on asking, seeking and knocking follow as commentary on the parable, the force of the Greek being 'keep on asking', 'keep on seeking', 'keep on knocking'. Jesus then directs attention to the human father, asking if he will give his child a snake for a fish or a scorpion for an egg, and so leads on to God himself who will surely give the Holy Spirit to those who ask him.

It is a mistake to think of petition, as some undoubtedly do, as an inferior form of prayer, suitable for children or newly converted Christians, which they will one day grow out of and leave behind. All of us use petition regularly in our daily offices, in the psalms, collects, versicles and responses and often in hymns, and perhaps it would be true for many to say they use it more frequently than they are aware. In the 119th psalm, for example, there are more than a hundred petitions. Eight occur in eight consecutive verses: 'Teach me, O Lord, the way of thy statutes', 'Incline my heart unto thy testimonies', 'Quicken me in thy righteousness', and so on.

Such petitionary prayers may be taken as examples of the type of petition most frequently on the lips of those who pray. It is possible that the person in the pew might not recognise them as petition. What such a one means by petition is perhaps only supplication for material and temporary blessings. It may be tempting to see such requests as belonging to a lower class of petition, but that is by no means necessarily so. It is circumstances that will determine what we should pray for. The appropriateness of any particular petitionary prayer is to be measured not by the nature of the gift sought but by the extent to which the prayer is directed to the glory of God.

Clearly petitionary prayer can have no place apart from a belief in personality in God. It has been said (truly, as I believe) that belief in personality in God could not long survive neglect in petitionary prayer. Put the other way round, it means that so long as our theology remains sound – witnessing to personality or something not less than personality within the being of God – we shall have the incentive to persist in petitionary prayer. When we use a personal pronoun for God, and either He or She would do equally well, we are affirming personality. We need not consider God personal in the sense in which we are personal. We may think of him as supra-personal but not non-personal which would reduce him to an 'it'. If God were an It, even the greatest of all possible Its, we should be his master and not he ours. Possibly we are in special danger of so reducing God in our times because we live in an age when the emphasis on God's immanence is not always balanced by his transcendence. Archbishop Michael Ramsey has some helpful words here: 'To call God He is to recognise that the Godhead has no less initiative than we have even though we know he has vastly more', and stressing the importance of balancing words like 'within' which stand for immanence and 'beyond' which stands for transcendence, he continues, 'Beyond, above, tell us of one upon whom we depend, who does things and initiates, whose perfection claims our allegiance, whose unlimitedness gives us littleness and awe. Here the image of Creator, Saviour, Judge comes home'. I think it true to say that so long as theology protects that imagery – an imagery which pervades the teaching of Jesus on the Father – so long and only so long will the petitionary importance of prayer remain.

1. There is just one exception: 1 Samuel 2:1ff.

∼7∼

Chronos and *Kairos* Prayer

The spiritual war

Finally, grow strong in the Lord, with the strength of his power. Put on the full armour of God so as to be able to resist the devil's tactics. For it is not against human enemies that we have to struggle, but against the principalities and the ruling forces who are masters of the darkness in this world, the spirits of evil in the heavens. That is why you must take up all God's armour, or you will not be able to put up any resistance on the evil day, or stand your ground even though you exert yourselves to the full.

So stand your ground, with truth a belt round your waist, and uprightness a breastplate, wearing for shoes on your feet the eagerness to spread the gospel of peace and always carrying the shield of faith so that you can use it to quench the burning arrows of the Evil One. And then you must take salvation as your helmet and the sword of the Spirit, that is, the word of God.

In all your prayer and entreaty keep praying in the Spirit on every possible occasion. Never get tired of staying awake to pray for all God's holy people, and pray for me to be given an opportunity to open my mouth and fearlessly make known the mystery of the gospel of which I am an ambassador in chains; pray that in proclaiming it I may speak as fearlessly as I ought to.

(Ephesians. 6:10–20)

In this epistle Paul tells us to put on the whole armour of God and reminds us that our warfare is not against 'flesh and blood' but against spiritual wickedness in high places. The various pieces of armour are described and we shall need them all. But with each one there is to be prayer. We are to pray always and it is this thought I will take here.

I recall reading some years ago an article which dealt with *kairos* and *chronos* times of prayer. *Kairos* and *chronos* are two Greek words meaning 'time' though they are not synonymous.

Kairos will generally refer to an appointed time or season whereas *chronos* stands for the duration of time, and from it comes our English word chronometer. *Kairos* is used in the New Testament in such verses as 'My time is at hand' or 'Watch and pray for you do not know the time when the Son of man will return'. Often in *kairos* there is a note of crisis whereas in *chronos* is simply the passing of the hour.

It is probably true to say that most people pray exclusively in *kairos* time whilst others pray mainly in the time described as *chronos* though they will use *kairos* as well. The *kairos* people are not to be despised but it is *chronos* people that God wants us to be. The *kairos* Christians are those who turn to God in times of special need or crisis, a bereavement or an illness or a disaster. Dr Johnson once asked a sailor home from a long voyage whether everything went well. 'Wonderfully,' he was assured, 'why, the weather was so calm that we only had to turn to prayer twice on the whole trip.' Those were *kairos* people.

People who are only of the *kairos* brand generally find prayer unrewarding when they turn to it. And naturally so. They may be likened to those who are taking their first swimming lesson after the boat has capsized. Whereas the *chronos* people have been doing their ten lengths in the pool daily, and in finding themselves unexpectedly in the sea they are, relatively speaking, unperturbed. For those who belong to *chronos*, prayer is a habit of life, it is the same for them whether the sun is shining or the storm clouds are gathering, their habit of prayer continues. For them there is the formation of regular daily practice, either alone or, as here, with others. From this there will come the overflow of prayer into work so that the whole of life, both in work and in prayer, becomes a continuous offering of love and thanksgiving.

This must be how Paul intended when he said we were to pray always. Only the *chronos* Christian who has regularly appointed times, come wind, come weather, can fulfil the apostolic command. It is natural that at times of crisis we should turn to prayer but the *kairos* person who prays only in times of necessity will be disappointed. The *kairos* prayer will be self-regarding. The one who uses it looks to be saved *from* disaster, whereas the *chronos* person looks to be held up *in* trial and temptation rather than to be saved from it.

It is only the *chronos* person who has the opportunity of making prayer an offering of love for it is his clock (or the community bell), and not his natural desires which take him to prayer. There are times when all of us experience the drawing to prayer and to follow that drawing is good and right. But that belongs to *kairos*, not to be despised, but it is not what Paul intended in the passage before us. At two o'clock in the morning most of us desire the warmth of the blankets rather than the cool of the chapel, and just because of that, a sacrificial offering of love presents itself. Those who, like myself, do not attempt the rigour of the night office can only admire others from afar. This is *chronos* prayer par excellence.

Let us close in making the point that prayer is above all an offering of love. 'At eventide,' said St John of the Cross 'they will examine you in love.' One of the dangers today in connection with prayer is to see it as being for our fulfilment or self-realisation. This is self-regarding and can only lead to a firmer entrenchment in self. Prayer is, of course, fulfilling and enlarging and all the rest – what else could communion with God be? – but it is as true in prayer as it is in life that he who loses his life shall find it. The paradox is that whilst God wants us to be fulfilled we shall not find fulfilment through seeking it. It comes through sacrifice, through the losing of life, and sacrifice is of the essence of *chronos* prayer. I think that, if we could see more clearly into the heart of things, we would be grateful for those times when we come to prayer with our hearts dry and our minds dulled, and all we can do is to sit or kneel and say 'Lord, I make this time an offering of love to you', and then just remain still for the appointed time. It is likely to seem a waste of time during the prayer period, but it is a safe rule in prayer that we are not to judge it by how it seems at the time but by its later fruits.

Our Need of Deliverance

Entering Jericho: the blind man

Now it happened that as he drew near to Jericho there was a blind
man sitting at the side of the road begging. When he heard the
crowd going past he asked what it was all about, and they told him
that Jesus the Nazarene was passing by. So he called out, 'Jesus, Son
of David, have pity on me.' The people in front scolded him and
told him to keep quiet, but he only shouted all the louder, 'Son of
David, have pity on me.' Jesus stopped and ordered them to bring
the man to him, and when he came up, asked him, 'What do you
want me to do for you?' 'Sir,' he replied, 'let me see again.' Jesus
said to him, 'Receive your sight. Your faith has saved you.' And
instantly his sight returned and he followed him praising God, and
all the people who saw it gave praise to God. (Luke 18:35–43)

As we approach Lent let us turn first to our epistle.[1] St Paul's
hymn of love, one of the most treasured passages, not only
in the Bible but in the literature of all time. It is by no accident
that this passage is brought before us at this time. Lent is
traditionally the season of fasting and other disciplines. The
epistle reminds us that nothing that we do has value in the sight
of God unless it is motivated by love. The collect is at pains to
make the same point: 'O Lord, who has taught us that all our
doings without charity are nothing worth . . .'

Our epistle takes us to the full flowering of the Christian life.
It is our gospel which takes us to its beginnings and for those
who have already begun it takes us to the place of continual
renewal. The cry of blind Bartimaeus – 'Jesus, son of David, have
mercy on me' – sprang from an awareness of desperate need,
and it refused to be silenced by the mistaken zeal of the disciples
for their master's comfort. We may suppose that Bartimaeus (we
learn his name from Mark's gospel) had often heard of the healer
of Nazareth, and perhaps he had often prayed that he would

23

meet him, and now he calls out with all his might, knowing perhaps that if this opportunity be lost his chance has gone for ever.

It may be there was more to it than just a sense of physical need – a guilt problem, perhaps, stretching into the distant past, making this a case of hysterical blindness – and if so this may have been first met in the warmth of the personality of Jesus which not even his blindness could conceal. But that is conjecture. At least we know that *our* problem is a spiritual one, that we need the continual outpouring of the mercy of Jesus if we are to be made whole. Our need, we know so well, is not just to be freed from our frailty and our weaknesses, but to be purged at the roots that our proud and independent natures may be overthrown. Yet, please God, in his time and not ours lest we be utterly undone. Only the mercy of God can effect this. Our own efforts are likely but to enmesh ourselves more firmly in the net in which we are caught.

How well I remember what must have been quite the most terrifying experience of my life. I was about twenty at the time, walking by the sea at low tide at the mouth of the River Exe. To my horror I began sinking in the mud. One's first instinct was to struggle but that only made things worse and I must have been nearly up to my knees before I realised the only thing to do was to stay still. But this was a lonely place and night was falling and the tide was coming in. You can imagine my relief when I saw two fishermen running towards me. I don't suppose I cried out aloud 'have mercy' but if ever there was such a cry in the heart it was mine at that time. With consummate skill they pulled me out. It is not a bad picture of our standing before God, our helplessness, our need of a deliverer, our faith that he can do what we can never do for ourselves. The psalmist has the same picture: 'Take me out of the mire that I sink not'.

So we need a deliverer. We need deliverance as persons and we need deliverance as a nation. Most of all, perhaps, we need deliverance from greed and covetousness. It is not poverty in itself which degrades – the world can offer many examples of material poverty combined with dignity of living – but covetousness and discontent. It cannot be the least of the services of places such as Bede House – and, thankfully there are many such pockets throughout our land – that they witness to the fact that

24

enough is enough, that the value of life is not to be measured in terms of the abundance of our possessions. One of the strange things about Cranmer's litany in our *Book of Common Prayer* is that it nowhere mentions the sin of covetousness. Perhaps he hardly dared include it as the old ships' captains made their voyages of plunder across the seas. Covetousness may be defined as an inordinate desire for that which is not one's own. Paul associates it (as does the tenth comandment) with sexual immorality as well as with material goods. In either case it is linked to offence against the person, the one more directly than the other. For which reason it would be shortsighted to separate the two in any analysis of our national plight.

'In all time of our tribulation; in all time of our wealth; in the hour of death, and in the day of judgement, *Good Lord, deliver us.*'[2]

1. 1 Corinthians 13; for scriptural text see No. 27.
2. From the litany of the *Book of Common Prayer.*

~9~

Forgiveness

Compassion and generosity

'Be compassionate just as your Father is compassionate. Do not judge, and you will not be judged; do not condemn, and you will not be condemned; forgive, and you will be forgiven. Give, and there will be gifts for you: a full measure, pressed down, shaken together, and overflowing, will be poured into your lap; because the standard you use will be the standard used for you.' (Luke 6:36–38)

I take words from our gospel passage (Luke 6:32–45): 'Forgive and you shall be forgiven'. We must have often reflected that the only clause in the Lord's Prayer with a condition attached is the one relating to forgiveness. It is also the only clause on which Jesus comments later: 'For if you do not forgive others their sins, neither will your heavenly Father forgive you'. Here in our gospel we have the same teaching, though in a positive form.

God's mercy is inexhaustible but it may often be that we raise barriers which prevent us being able to take it into ourselves. Chief of these is the spirit of unforgivingness. If we say that we cannot forgive another God can deal with that. The implication is that we would like to forgive but that we find ourselves unable to do so. God can then work on our desire as we pray for this person in obedience to the words of Jesus (Matthew 5:44–45) and eventually bring it to fulfilment. But if we say that we will not forgive that would seem to present an insuperable problem to God since he has chosen to give us free will. The one who wilfully persists in unforgivingness automatically excludes themself from heaven. Such a one can never be in heaven, not by an arbitrary decision of God, but simply because heaven would no longer be heaven if such a person were to slip in.

The Father's mercy is inexhaustible and it is only the barriers that we erect which can prevent it from reaching us. 'Be merciful,' our gospel opens, 'as your Father is merciful.' Matthew's equivalent is 'Be perfect, as your Father is perfect'. Taking the two together we might say the Father's perfection lies in the inexhaustibility of his mercy. Nowhere is this represented more vividly than in a parable related only by Luke, the parable of the prodigal son. The boy who had squandered his father's money was welcomed home, embraced, clothed, fed and forgiven with never a word of blame. Moreover he learnt that his sonship had never lapsed.

It is psychologically impossible to accept God's forgiveness for oneself without extending this same spirit of forgiveness to one's neighbour. Equally is this true if my neighbour is the closest of all possible neighbours, my own deepest self. Jesus said that we must love our neighbours as ourselves and so it must follow that we are to love ourselves as our neighbour. We are not to love ourselves, as doubtless we often do, with an indulgent pampering love, any more than we are to love our neighbour with a love of that nature. We are to love ourselves with the same strength and insistence as God's love, and that means we are to have the same generosity towards ourselves as we have towards others.

For many good and conscientious people this can be the most difficult part of forgiveness. 'Come, my soul, we are fallen into a ditch' is the gentle admonishment of St Francis de Sales. But such admonishment does not come naturally. Wounded pride will reveal itself in impatience, hurt feelings and in some natures a temper of mind akin to despair. 'What right,' we say, 'have we to forgive ourselves?' It is the wrong question. If God has forgiven us, what right have we not to forgive ourselves? Father Harry Williams of the Community of the Resurrection pointed this out vividly in a recent broadcast talk. 'No right at all,' he concluded, 'for it is nonsense to suppose we should defy our creator by hating the creature whom he himself loves with an intensity and depth which only the cross of Jesus can adequately reveal.'

∾ 10 ∾

Offering

Taking as our theme the offering of life, I would like to speak of this especially in relation to prayer. The subject of prayer could be approached from many angles, of which the aspect of offering is but one – not of course offering standing in isolation from the rest of life, but as a part of our total self-offering to God. The psalm writer of old speaks on this aspect of prayer when he writes: 'I will offer unto thee the sacrifice of thanksgiving, and call upon the name of the Lord', and the same thought is given Christian content in the Epistle to the Hebrews (13:15) where we read: 'Through Jesus Christ let us continually offer up to God the sacrifice of praise, that is the tribute of the lips which acknowledges his name.'

In both passages it is the vocal offering which the writers have in mind and for us this will find one main expression in the singing of the offices. But equally the offering applies to silent prayer which Evelyn Underhill describes in *Worship* as a speechless self-offering, a total oblation of personality, and uses the image of the burnt offering to express the total self-loss of the creature in its Home and Father, which is the consummation of worship.

However the offering may be made, we do well to remind ourselves that we do not make it alone. It is, as the writer to the Hebrews says, made 'through Jesus', and so, too, in union with his mystical body, the Church, and we are enabled to make it, not through our own strength, but through the action of the Holy Spirit. The offering is ours, for God does not over-ride our freedom, but it is ours in response to grace, a response freely and gladly given.

If we are able to see prayer quite simply as an offering, one important consequence will follow. We shall be relieved of all anxiety to make prayer successful, whatever that may mean. Is my prayer strengthening? Ignore it. Offerings are simply to be offered. Is my prayer doing any good? Dash the thought to the ground. If the prayer be offered, that is enough.

That offerings sometimes go wrong was brought home to me as a small boy when I bought my father what was to me a beautiful earthenware vase. Early on his birthday morning I laid it on his bed so that it should be the first thing he looked upon when he woke up. Alas, when I went to share his delight, there it was in a hundred pieces on the floor. Naturally my credulity was strained to the uttermost when he said he would value the pieces just as much, but we can understand. I suppose our prayers are often like that broken jar, fragmented, imperfect, lying before God in a hundred pieces, and yet if the offering be made gladly and lovingly, they are accepted and treasured in a manner beyond our imagining. Dryness, desolation, involuntary distraction, confusion, none of this can destroy prayer if the offering remains. When Paul said that God loves a cheerful giver he surely meant that to be applied to all life and not simply to almsgiving.

It is a mark of maturity that we should have our regular times of prayer which we keep independently of inner mood or consciousness of need. And it is these times, often coming at moments when we would much prefer to do something else, which especially supply prayer with this element of offering. Particularly will this be so for you in the night office. The last thing you may feel like doing at two o'clock on a winter morning is to leave your warm beds, walk through the chilly garden to this chapel, and spend an hour in prayer and praise. There must be days when you can't feel like praising, but no matter, the offering is there, and with that God is well pleased. And in some way beyond our understanding, and especially if we are not thinking about it, or not wanting to help it happen, but remain rooted in the desire to make an acceptable offering to God, the quality of life is raised for us all.

～11～

The Stilling of the Storm

The calming of the storm

It happened that one day he got into a boat with his disciples and said to them, 'Let us cross over to the other side of the lake.' So they set out, and as they sailed he fell asleep. When a squall of wind came down on the lake the boat started shipping water and they found themselves in danger. So they went to rouse him saying, 'Master! Master! We are lost!' Then he woke up and rebuked the wind and the rough water; and they subsided and it was calm again. He said to them, 'Where is your faith?' They were awestruck and astounded and said to one another, 'Who can this be, that gives orders even to winds and waves and they obey him?' (Luke 8:22–25)

Our gospel brings before us the stilling of the storm on the Lake of Galilee (Luke 8:22–39). There are many in the Church today who would want to modify the account we have received. They would say that our Lord's confidence and serenity when he was awakened by the disciples communicated itself to them so that the wind and the waves, which seemed so threatening before, lost their power to disturb the disciples' agitated minds. What had seemed to be a threatening tempest appeared now to be little more than a trifling squall. One can imagine how indignant seasoned fishermen like Peter and James and John would have been if someone of their own day had tried to fob them off with this sort of explanation.

I remember running into a severe storm many years ago as we were flying over the Caribbean sea. To the passenger sitting near me I suppose I must have looked alarmed as we plunged and lurched and watched the hand baggage being tossed off the rack on to the floor or on to ourselves. At any rate he turned to me and told me that he was a pilot, that he had been through many storms and that this was really quite a slight affair and that there was no need for alarm. Undoubtedly his own composure

30

improved my morale and I became confident that all was well. But I was not so dimwitted as to be unaware that the luggage continued to fall, that the lightning still appeared to be striking our wing tips, that the plane continued to heave and roll. No doubt the presence of Jesus awake in the boat gave the disciples hope, as my fellow passenger gave me confidence, but to attempt to explain away the stilling of the storm in the terms I have outlined would be quite unrealistic. I knew the storm continued to rage and so did the disciples until he commanded it to cease.

I think we may learn a valuable lesson – perhaps many valuable lessons – from today's story. I want to consider just one point today, that there is a sense in which Jesus worked this miracle unwillingly. The impression is irresistible that the better way would have been for the disciples to have passed through the storm confidently and courageously, and that the miracle was worked as a concession to their weakness. 'Why are you fearful? How is it that you have no faith?' I draw, too, on Mark's account.

What is it we have to learn? All of us have to be taken into the storm as the disciples were that day. The storm may be an operation or a rejection or a bereavement. It may be insidious and subtle temptation, or violent temptation, or a frustration of our hopes, or a change of fortune or many other things. Whatever it is, God could remove this obstacle, this trial which presses so heavily upon us, by an act of power, as Jesus stilled the winds and the waves on the Galilean lake. And sometimes he does remove the storm, and we may praise him for it, for he knows best. But it may be that his primary will for us is, as was his primary will for his disciples, not that the storm should be removed but that we should pass through it with untroubled hearts and our faith intact.

I recall the case of a woman of remarkable faith and character who worked as a matron in a school I was serving in India. I remember the day when she told me that she had been diagnosed as suffering from cancer, and that she would have to leave the school for a period to undergo an operation and treatment. We had a special service of intercession for her and many remarked on the Spirit's power on that occasion. I have no doubt that God could have arrested the cancer and reversed the decaying process by a single act of power had he so willed, but he chose not to remove the storm but to see her through it. I had a letter from her – I wish I had it now – telling of the indescribable peace and sense of God's protecting love as she awaited her operation in the ward and then on the operating table. She was out of the hospital in less than half the expected time – no doubt her deep trust and acceptance assisted her recovery – and she lived for another thirty years. May we not believe that God wrought a deeper service for this person by drawing out her faith and courage, and our faith and love – seeing her through the storm – than would have been possible if the storm had been removed?

It may be that we often get our priorities wrong in these matters. We look for our storms to be removed whereas God would have us pass through them in serenity and trust. For the one who had built their house upon the rock of the gospel we are not told that they would be protected from storm and tempest. We are told rather that when the rain fell, and the floods came, and the storm raged that the house remained standing. That was their reward: the house stood firm. In the words of the Lady Julian of Norwich: 'He said not, "thou shalt not be tempested" but he said, "thou shalt not be overcome." '

Pilgrimage to Christ

The visit of the Magi

After Jesus had been born at Bethlehem in Judaea during the reign of King Herod, suddenly some wise men came to Jerusalem from the east asking, 'Where is the infant king of the Jews? We saw his star as it rose and have come to do him homage.' When King Herod heard this he was perturbed, and so was the whole of Jerusalem. He called together all the chief priests and the scribes of the people, and enquired of them where the Christ was to be born. They told him, 'At Bethlehem in Judaea, for this is what the prophet wrote:

> And you, Bethlehem, in the land of Judah,
> you are by no means the least among the leaders of Judah,
> for from you will come a leader
> who will shepherd my people Israel.'

Then Herod summoned the wise men to see him privately. He asked them the exact date on which the star had appeared and sent them on to Bethlehem with the words, 'Go and find out all about the child, and when you have found him, let me know, so that I too may go and do him homage.' Having listened to what the king had to say, they set out. And suddenly the star they had seen rising went forward and halted over the place where the child was. The sight of the star filled them with delight, and going into the house they saw the child with his mother Mary, and falling to their knees they did him homage. Then, opening their treasures, they offered him gifts of gold and frankincense and myrrh. But they were given a warning in a dream not to go back to Herod, and returned to their own country by a different way. (Matthew 2:1–12)

All the world knows and loves the story of which this gospel reading speaks. The Christmas cards alone ensure that it shall never be forgotten. There they are – these men – on the cards I have received, mounted sedately on their camels, serenely making their way across the desert, the star shining before them above the brightness of the setting sun. Or perhaps they have arrived at the manger and are seen to be bowing in homage before the young child, presenting their gifts of gold and frankincense and myrrh. Here is a theme which offers endless possibilities of richness and depth for poetry and art and drama.

Often, I suspect, we think we know more about these men than we actually do. I suppose that almost all would say, for a start, that there were three of them, and be surprised to learn that the Bible does not give their number, which is simply an inference from the gifts they brought. And again, perhaps, many of us imagine – once more from the Christmas cards – that they came alone. But this is most unlikely in a world where people in a quite modest position were surrounded by a retinue of servants, and where the dangers and hardships by the way would have made a lone journey almost impossible. We never see them, I fancy, these three finely clothed men on our cards, caught in a desert sandstorm and halted, miserable and exhausted, until it had blown itself out; or parched under the scorching desert sun, searching wearily for a haven where they might find rest and water; or held up by rivers in flood, or struggling through difficult terrain; or delayed by threat of brigands or beasts of prey. It is likely that some at least of these hazards would have been encountered on the way.

However it may have been with these men, we know that our pilgrimage cannot be symbolised by tranquil journeys under clear skies, the way before us made plain by the never-failing star leading us on. For us there have been the dry and painful periods symbolised by the desert sands under the relentless eastern sun, such as the psalm writer must have known when he likened himself to a wineskin cracked and dried and seemingly of little use. Or there have been days symbolised by robbers in the way, threatening to halt our journey, or at least to impede our progress and cheat us of much we hold dear. Even more threatening have been the storms which arise from our tempestuous nature, or from the depression and bewilderment which sometimes un-accountably take hold of us, our share perhaps in those evils which the craft and subtlety of the devil or our own fallen nature works against us. 'My soul is among lions' says the psalmist, referring to those who threatened to tear him apart by backbiting, accusation and slander.

Whatever form our pigrimage may take, we know that it can never be without hardship, though in God's time there will be resting places where we can be refreshed for the renewal of our task. As the pilgrims of old made their way to the holy city they found that even Bitter Valley could be made into a place of springs to be covered with the blessing of the autumn rains.[1]

But we would not have it otherwise. You may remember how King David wished to set up an altar on the threshing floor of Araunah. Araunah would gladly have given the king not only the threshing floor but the oxen to be sacrificed. Yet David insisted on making payment, saying, 'I will not offer to the Lord that which has cost me nothing'. I suppose these are words which may often find an echo in our hearts as we go to our work, or our prayers, or fulfill our duties to one another, not to mention the inner trials which belong to each one of us on the way. 'I will not offer to the Lord that which has cost me nothing.' (2 Samuel 24:24).

1. Psalm 84:8 (Grail translation).

13

Encountering Jesus

> Now there was a woman who had suffered from a haemorrhage for twelve years; after long and painful treatment under various doctors, she had spent all she had without being any the better for it; in fact, she was getting worse. She had heard about Jesus, and she came up through the crowd and touched his cloak from behind, thinking, 'If I can just touch his clothes, I shall be saved.' And at once the source of the bleeding dried up, and she felt in herself that she was cured of her complaint. And at once aware of the power that had gone out from him, Jesus turned round in the crowd and said, 'Who touched my clothes?' His disciples said to him, 'You see how the crowd is pressing round you; how can you ask, "Who touched me?" ' But he continued to look all round to see who had done it. Then the woman came forward, frightened and trembling because she knew what had happened to her, and she fell at his feet and told him the whole truth. 'My daughter,' he said, 'your faith has restored you to health; go in peace and be free of your complaint.'
>
> (Mark 5:25–34)

Our gospel speaks of the healing of Jairus' daughter (Mark 5:21–43). It is not, however, of that that I wish to speak but of an incident on the way, the healing of the woman suffering from a haemorrhage over the past twelve years.

In what frame of mind did she come to Jesus? It must be that she came in hope. She had known hope before but not in him. She had seen many doctors. Hope would surge up only to be disappointed. Indeed, far from getting better, Mark tells us she grew worse, a detail omitted by Luke who as a doctor would naturally have been sensitive on that point. There are so many things in which people put their hope – wealth, social status, education, health and much more. Happy are we if our hope is in God alone, or, if in earthly things, then in these as being derived from him, so that our hope is not fixed in them but in

God who is beyond. Our lives may be seen as a pilgrimage in hope, a disengagement from hope in transitory things which cannot ultimately satisfy, for the putting on of a strong and courageous hope in God that he will bring to completion the work he has begun. God is faithful, says St Paul, and will sustain us to the end, presenting us blameless in the day of Jesus Christ. And so it is that the God of hope will fill us with all joy and peace in believing.

Secondly, this woman came in faith; indeed her faith is singled out and commended. 'Go in peace,' says Jesus. 'Your faith has healed you.' But a further point is given for our consideration. In spite of the fact that the crowd is pressing on Jesus from all sides he is aware that he has been approached by someone in special need. 'Someone has touched me, for power has gone from me.' Faith cannot stand alone, it has to be faith in someone or something. This was no auto-suggestive cure, the mere action of the mind over the body. It was the reception of a gift from another, though faith laid the woman open to receive that gift. This is a thought we may take with us to the reception of our communion. There are some whose emphasis at such times is in the disposition of the receiver, others for whom the stress is overwhelmingly on the reality of the gift, 'the body and blood of Christ, verily and indeed, taken and received by the faithful in the Lord's supper'. You will notice how that quotation from the catechism combines the objective and the subjective, referring both to the gift and the faith which receives it. We cannot separate these two. As well might you try to separate teaching and listening in the process of learning. The best teacher could teach nothing if the pupil did not listen, and the best pupil would learn nothing if the teacher did not teach. Or to use another example: food would be useless without a digestion to assimilate it and a digestion would be of no use without a meal to feed it. This woman truly received a gift from Jesus and her faith enabled her to appropriate it.

And thirdly, she came humbly and longingly with a deep sense of her need which only he could supply. There were others who drew near to Jesus, indeed, as we have seen, they pressed upon him, but we do not imagine that the mere fact of physical close-ness became an occasion for blessing. That blessing was available only to those who shared this woman's expectancy and longing. Our thoughts turn today to how this woman came to Jesus, humbly, longingly, faithfully, hopefully and lovingly, bringing to him the fullness of her need. It is for this grace that we ask as we prepare to meet our Lord today. 'Come, Lord, with the dawning of the day. Make yourself known in the breaking of the bread, for you are our God for ever and ever.'

⁓14⁓

The Rich Man and Lazarus

The parable of the rich man and Lazarus

'There was a rich man who used to dress in purple and fine linen and feast magnificently every day. And at his gate there used to lie a poor man called Lazarus, covered with sores, who longed to fill himself with what fell from the rich man's table. Even dogs came and licked his sores. Now it happened that the poor man died and was carried away by the angels into Abraham's embrace. The rich man also died and was buried.

'In his torment in Hades he looked up and saw Abraham a long way off with Lazarus in his embrace. So he cried out, "Father Abraham, pity me and send Lazarus to dip the tip of his finger in water and cool my tongue, for I am in agony in these flames." Abraham said, "My son, remember that during your life you had your fill of good things, just as Lazarus his fill of bad. Now he is being comforted here while you are in agony. But that is not all: between us and you a great gulf has been fixed, to prevent those who want to cross from our side to yours or from your side to ours."

'So he said, "Father, I beg you then to send Lazarus to my father's house, since I have five brothers, to give them warning so that they do not come to this place of torment too." Abraham said, "They have Moses and the prophets, let them listen to them." The rich man replied, "Ah no, father Abraham, but if someone comes to them from the dead, they will repent." Then Abraham said to him. "If they will not listen either to Moses or to the prophets, they will not be convinced even if someone should rise from the dead." '

(Luke 16:19–31)

The parable of Dives and Lazarus set before us in the gospel reading brings home the responsibility of wealth. Riches are generally suspect in the New Testament but nowhere are they taught to be wrong in themselves and today's parable has something other to say to us than that. For to begin with the parable does not speak to us of the poor – the economically poor in general, but of one particular poor man, a pauper indeed in his absence of worldly goods, yet one who in spite of the cruelty of his state was not hardened nor embittered, but maintained throughout his trust in God. That I think we can rightly deduce from the fact that Jesus gave this man a name, which is the more significant in that in no other parable is anyone so portrayed. It may be said that the story required a proper name, but it is significant that the name given was Lazarus, which is the Greek form of the Hebrew Eleazar, meaning 'God is my helper'.

If one may be allowed to make the remark without presumption, Jesus is far more perceptive in calling the poor man Lazarus than we are in giving the name of Dives to the other, for that name has application simply to his external state. We have in fact robbed the name given by Jesus of its spiritual association for Lazarus nowadays means leper or beggar and of course the word *lazaretto* is directly derived from it. So that when now we use the name Lazarus (with its altered meaning) we deprive the parable of an important insight, namely that Lazarus eventually found himself in heaven not because he had been poor but because in his poverty he had put his hope in God.

It may be tedious to press the point further but it is hard to pass over the teasing spectacle at the end of the parable – for it must be teasing to reformers who see the equal distribution of wealth as the cure to social evils – the glimpse we are given of earth's poorest man locked in eternal embrace with Father Abraham, who according to the Bible was the richest man of his day. Here in this parable we have the richest man on earth not simply getting to heaven but being represented as heaven itself! Without wishing to be provocative let me say we do well to stand firmly against Christian people – though we may find more compelling grounds than this – who want to reduce Jesus to the level of a social reformer instead of seeing him as being primarily concerned with people's dispositions and motives. Here we have the spectacle of the world's richest man and the world's poorest man set together in heaven not on account of the presence or absence of possessions upon earth, but simply because the life of each was rooted in trust in God. But before I go too far down this road let me recall the paradox of poverty as stated by C. S. Lewis: poverty is blessed and must always be relieved.

The New Testament, as we know, and the teaching of Jesus in particular, is plentiful in its warnings of the deceitfulness of riches. It has been said that 'our Lord represents the ministry of wealth as one of the dangerous trades in which there is a high rate of spiritual mortality'. We recall the parable of the rich fool (Luke 12:13–21), and indeed this parable we are reading today, and we recall how Jesus said it was easier for a camel to go through a needle's eye than for a rich man to enter heaven. Although Mark reduces the force of the teaching by saying that Jesus referred to those who *trust* in riches, it is generally agreed that this is a later gloss.

The rich man, we are told, had his good things in this life. There is nothing wrong in that. We may all have good things here and now. The trouble begins when possessiveness is present, when the attitude of ownership replaces that of stewardship. If Jesus appears to single out wealth as a root of evil it is because riches have such an insiduous corrupting power over our whole nature, predisposing us to possessiveness and all that goes with it, selfishness, superiority, callousness – in a word pride, which in essence means seeing one as master of one's destiny.

I suppose that all who have taken the vows of the religious life must sometimes reflect on how easy would be the struggle if it ended with the renunciation of earthly possessions. For it is as possible to enter into proprietorship within a community as in the world outside. It will no longer be my wealth which is the issue but perhaps instead my time, my period of silence, my friendships. St John of the Cross warns against attachment to spiritual things and comments that if a bird is prevented from flight it matters not whether it is held back by a rope or a thread. The climax of this process is reached in the gospel story where Jesus says that his own continuing presence in the flesh is holding his disciples back because of their reliance on him and so it is desirable that he should leave them. In the words of Meister Eckhart, it is as though he said, 'You have taken too much joy in my physical presence, hence the perfect joy of the Holy Spirit cannot be imparted to you. Therefore detachment is necessary for us all, detachment which purifies the soul, cleanses the conscience, inflames the heart, arouses the spirit, quickens desire and makes God known in union with himself.'

41

～15～

Acceptance of Forgiveness

Seeing that their father was dead, Joseph's brothers said, 'What if Joseph intends to treat us as enemies and pay us back for all the wrong we did him?' So they sent this message to Joseph: 'Before your father died, he gave us this order: "You are to say to Joseph: Now please forgive the crime and faults of your brothers and all the wrong they did you." So now please forgive the crime of the servants of your father's God.' Joseph wept at the message they sent to him.

Then his brothers went to him themselves and, throwing themselves at his feet, said, 'Take us as your slaves!' But Joseph replied, 'Do not be afraid; is it for me to put myself in God's place? The evil you planned to do me has by God's design been turned to good, to bring about the present result: the survival of a numerous people. So there is no need to be afraid, I shall provide for you and your dependants.' In this way he reassured them by speaking affectionately to them. (Genesis 50:15–21)

The story of Joseph, of which we have read a part in our first lesson (Genesis 45:1–15), is one of the best loved of the biblical sagas. Some stories are little more than a succession of incidents but this is a unity and should be taken as a whole. We are irresistibly carried forward with the unfolding events narrated with great dramatic power. And it is a story with great depth of spiritual teaching. Take, for example, the words in today's reading: 'God sent me before you. So it was not you who sent me but God.' (Genesis 45:8). How many sermons on the overruling Providence of God must not have been preached on the experience of Joseph, betrayed by his brothers, sold into slavery and yet preserved by God to be a ruler in Egypt, and more than that, to be a man of great integrity, of winning graciousness as he returns good for evil, becoming the reconciler of his brothers.

Yet it is not this of which I want to speak – at least not directly of this – but of a later incident (described in the extract above) which took place after the death of Joseph's father, Jacob. We read that the brothers of Joseph, having received his full forgiveness, said to one another after Jacob's death: 'Perhaps Joseph will now hate us and pay us back for all the evil we did to him. So they sent a message to him saying: "Your father before he died told us to ask you to forgive us for all the wrong we did to you. Now we pray that you forgive us our wickedness".' We read that on hearing this Joseph broke down and cried. 'Don't be afraid,' he replied, 'I will provide for you and your little ones.'

Nothing can have been more gracious than Joseph's forgiveness of his brothers. Listen again to these words, so moving, so artlessly simple: 'Joseph said to his brothers, "Come near to me, I pray you". And they came near and he said: "I am your brother Joseph whom you sold into Egypt. And now do not be distressed or angry with yourselves because you sold me here, for God has sent me before you to preserve life. So you see, my brothers, it wasn't really you who sent me here but God. Now go to my father and say "Come down. Don't delay. You and your children shall be near me, and all that you have. I will provide for you". And he kissed them and wept on them.'

How is it then that after such magnanimity these same men are filled with fear after their father's death? So frightened are they that they cannot go straight to Joseph asking for forgiveness – not that that would have been necessary since they were already forgiven – but they decide instead to make up a story, putting the responsibility upon Jacob, saying that he had told them to come to Joseph in this way. I suppose that they thought that Joseph had forgiven them simply for their father's sake, and that now that Jacob was dead the forgiveness would be withdrawn and their sins would be rolled back on them. And what of Joseph? He told them not to be afraid and promised to look after them.

We have a gracious God. Throughout scripture runs the golden thread of a merciful God abounding in steadfast love and faithfulness. 'Turn unto the Lord your God for he is gracious and full of compassion,' says the prophet Joel. 'Who is a God like unto thee that pardoneth iniquity?' says Micah. And what has been foreshadowed in the prophets has been brought to completion in Christ.

May it be sometimes that the mercy of God is too much for us, just as Joseph's graciousness was too much for his guilty brothers? 'So deeply', it has been said, 'had the consciousness of guilt entered into their heart that hardly anything could wash it clean. So profoundly was their outlook affected that it was impossible for them to look at goodness and see it cleanly and clearly for what it was.' These brothers were unknowingly belittling Joseph in doubting his forgiveness. Just so do we dishonour God if we go back anxiously with unquiet minds over our past sins as though he had not forgiven us. We must try to be objective, not to look at the past as these brothers did from within the limitation of their own characters, whereas their minds should have been fastened on the character of Joseph. 'Remember not the sins of my youth', and if we find ourselves echoing this cry let it not be with fearfulness or mistrust. As the goodness of Joseph was far beyond what his brothers could imagine, so is God's goodness far beyond our conception. Not by searching into our own hearts shall we see it, but by looking out into the revelation of him in Jesus, and grasping this, holding fast to it in faith. 'For my thoughts are not your thoughts,' says the Lord, 'and my ways are not your ways For as the heavens are higher than the earth so are my ways higher than your ways and my thoughts than your thoughts.' (Isaiah 55:8–9).

So let us learn from this that we must accept forgiveness and restoration into fellowship with God in simplicity and trust as little children, not wearily going over the years the locust has eaten, but placing our faith and hope in God's redeeming work in Christ whereby, says St Peter, 'we have been brought out of darkness into his marvellous light, which in time past were not a people but are now the people of God, which had not obtained mercy but now have obtained mercy' (1 Peter 2:9–10).

The Fruit of the Spirit

> The fruit of the Spirit is love, joy, peace, patience, kindness, goodness, trustfulness, gentleness and self-control: no law can touch such things as these. All who belong to Christ have crucified self with all its passions and its desires. Since we are living by the Spirit, let our behaviour be guided by the Spirit and let us not be conceited or provocative and envious of one another. (Galatians 5:22–26)

The fruit of the Spirit is love, joy, peace, patience, kindness goodness, faithfulness, gentleness, self-control. There is music in these words, and merely to repeat them and linger upon them is in itself a kind of mental and spiritual therapy. Especially is this so of the first three – love, joy, peace – words whose very sound seems to convey the qualities they express. Let us think in particular of the second of these fruits, joy – spiritual joy – and at once we shall be linked with the dominant note in the gospel passage: thanksgiving. We recall how one of the ten lepers returned to give thanks (Luke 17:15–16). It is the grateful people who are the happy people, and where gratitude is absent we look in vain for joy.

Joy – sensible, felt joy – belongs to the emotional side of our natures and, as we know so well, our emotions are not directly and immediately under the control of our wills. And so it is not in our power to feel joy by an act of the will any more than we are able to experience the feeling of love or peace or gratitude as and when we might wish. Sometimes it seems to us that joy is bubbling up within us as from some interior spring, but there are other times when the spring appears to have dried up, and the emotional side of our nature is marked at best with dryness, at worst with gloom and heaviness and depression. This must be the experience of everyone. Does it mean that we have failed, that we are failing in our Christian vocation, that in some way we are blocking the Spirit in the work he would do in us?

45

To answer that question I think we must consider another word which finds constant expression in the scriptures. If there is a lot about joy, there is no less about what we might call its companion word – rejoice or rejoicing. These two words – joy, the noun, and the verb, rejoice – supplement one another. There is this important distinction between them, that whereas joy belongs to the emotions, rejoicing belongs to the will. It is not in our power to feel joy at the command of the will, but it is in our power to rejoice in so far as we are free people aided by grace. There will be times when joy will overflow in rejoicing, as did the leper's joy when he saw he was healed and returned to glorify God and to give thanks; there are other times, and for many they will be the more usual ones when we must first rejoice – this is the act of the will – and then in the long run, and not by any means necessarily immediately, the emotions will follow the direction of the will. To rejoice, to make rejoicing the habitual attitude of life, is the sowing and nurturing of the seed, which yields the fruit of the Spirit which we know as joy.

There is, we know, a great deal about rejoicing in the New Testament, and sometimes it takes place in the most unlikely situations. Rejoicing overflows into the adverse circumstances of life only because our lives are at their centre anchored in a deep hope in what God in Christ has done and is doing both in ourselves and in others. It is when our lives are rooted in Christ, and indeed as they become firmly rooted in him, that the rejoicing which is centred in his redemptive activity can extend to all the circumstances of life, even to those which are most seemingly adverse and hostile. This is where Christian heroism begins, where the tried soldier, yet more the disciplined veteran, is distinguished from the raw recruit. So the apostles, threatened and ill-treated, depart rejoicing that they have been counted worthy to suffer for his name; or in prison Paul and Silas, their feet fastened in the stocks, rejoice at midnight with songs of praise.

Yet we all know how hard it is to rejoice even in the slight irritations or setbacks or frustrations which are presented to us in the course of daily living, let alone in the more difficult situations of injury or illness, depression or pressing temptation, or persistent fear, or, for many people, an unhappy marriage or home situation to which seemingly there is no solution. Is there any practical advice we can offer? Yes, I think that at least this can be said, that we may need to work at acceptance before rejoicing is possible in any situation which cannot, or cannot for the time being, be changed. But I would want to add that just as acceptance prepares the way for rejoicing, so rejoicing will help us to accept.

'The joy of the Lord is your strength.' So wrote Nehemiah and do we not all know that so much can be done in the spirit of joy which otherwise must remain unaccomplished? Spiritual joy is not the prerogative of a happy nature; in fact it may well be that people of sunny disposition, as we call it, are at a disadvantage compared with those of a naturally melancholy temperament. You may remember how von Hugel speaks of the Abbé Huvelin – 'himself of most melancholy natural temperament and full of mental and physical suffering' who yet radiated 'a tonic joy'. Harder it is for people of a naturally buoyant temperament, for the danger then is to rest in a purely natural happiness rather than plunging into that death which releases a supernatural joy, in the power of which (I quote Father Benson) we are to be made triumphant in temptation and trial. For joy supplies us with great strength. 'It is a law of our nature,' Father Benson continues, 'that the joy of the mind supplies the strength of the body, and that which we do with gladness we can do to a manifold greater degree than that which we can do with the mere muscular effort of the outer frame. So the joy of God enables us to do manifold things which would otherwise overpower us.'

～17～

Humility

To the faithful

In the same way, younger people, be subject to the elders. Humility towards one another must be the garment you all wear constantly, because God opposes the proud but accords his favour to the humble. Bow down, then, before the power of God now, so that he may raise you up in due time; unload all your burden on to him, since he is concerned about you. Keep sober and alert, because your enemy the devil is on the prowl like a roaring lion, looking for someone to devour. Stand up to him, strong in faith and in the knowledge that it is the same kind of suffering that the community of your brothers throughout the world is undergoing. You will have to suffer only for a little while: the God of all grace who called you to eternal glory in Christ will restore you, he will confirm, strengthen and support you. His power lasts for ever and ever. Amen.

(1 Peter 5:5–11)

At this St Peter's tide let us consider a few verses from Peter's epistle (1 Peter 5:1–11). 'Clothe yourselves always with humility towards one another.' Commentators tell us that the Greek word used here for 'clothe' occurs nowhere else in the New Testament. It is an interesting word, making the literal meaning of our text to be, 'Put on the apron of humility', the apron being the garment worn by slaves, marking out their menial status. Jesus would have so 'girded himself' at the Last Supper as he prepared to wash the disciples' feet. The incident made a great impression on Peter, who at first protested vehemently at being thus served by his Lord and master. The apron of the slave may have remained vividly in his mind, accounting for the unusual Greek word used for 'clothe' in this passage.

Humility is an elusive virtue. The New Testament bids us to be humble and to humble ourselves under God's hands but nowhere does it tell us to seek humility. That must be because seeking for humility is likely to be counter-productive, the danger being that we shall congratulate ourselves on the so-called humility we believe ourselves to have found. And so instead of possessing 'the queen of all the graces' we are even more firmly established in the pride we had hoped to overthrow. Humility does not come that way. It is a grace which steals in quietly and unawares as our attention is engaged elsewhere.

Yet Peter does not leave us without guidance as to how we may be clothed with this most lovely of garments. The key is in verse 7 of our epistle: 'Casting all your care upon him for he careth for you'. Humility is the child of trust, and trust means dependence in contrast to the 'go it alone' spirit which is the hallmark of pride. 'Humble yourselves,' says Peter, 'under the mighty hand of God', which I take to mean that in trial and contradiction, sorrow and sickness, we are to endure patiently until the time of our deliverance is at hand. Humility has been called the daughter of patience. Yet (it has been well said) we do best to see humilty not as a separate virtue but as a quality which suffuses every virtue thereby enabling it to be its true self. Thus patience (so-called) without humility is not true patience; generosity (so-called) without humility is not true generosity; goodness (so-called) without humility is not true goodness. And so we might go on.

Life provides many opportunities for humbling ourselves. The occasions will vary depending on who we are and the circumstances in which our lives are set. But common to every life is the humbling of ourselves in the acceptance of God's forgiveness of our sins. The cross of Christ is the breaking point of pride. It has often been said that Satan finds nothing so hard to bear as the sign of the cross. That is because Satan embodies the principle of pride and its overthrow is in the cross. Here in the cross is the invitation to everyone who thirsts, to him who has no money, to come to the waters to be refreshed with wine and milk, without money and without price (Isaiah 55:1). The trouble is we want to produce our purses, to present our credentials, but God says, 'no, no, not that'. The sacrifices of God are a troubled spirit – a broken and a contrite heart, O God, thou wilt not despise. Those are the words of David and he came to them through an agony of soul as he fasted and prayed that the life of the ill-conceived son of himself and Bathsheba might be spared. In one way or another we all have to descend to the valley of humiliation, several deep valleys perhaps, but many lesser ones. Yet the valley gives way to the hills as we come to accept (in the words of the collect) 'that we have no power of ourselves to help ourselves' and cast ourselves on the mercy of God as our only ground of hope. It is in such moments that humility slips in silently by the back door as we learn to take freely the grace of forgiveness which God holds out to us all.

It is in coming to God as we are, with pretences removed, and freely allowing him to accept us as we are, that we become clothed with the apron of humility. And be it noted that as soon after as we return to the memory of our wrongdoing in a spirit of blaming ourselves for it, we have begun to remove the apron and to return to the false satisfaction, wherein pride once more lifts up its head. It is a strange paradox that we long for peace, and yet cannot resist indulging ourselves in the rotten satisfaction of returning to the self-blame which dispels it. We deceive ourselves into believing we are honouring God, whereas in reality we are dishonouring him in denying the generosity of his love.

> Just as I am, without one plea,
> But that thy blood was shed for me,
> And that thou bidd'st me come to thee,
>   O Lamb of God, I come.

~18~

Recognising Jesus

We are told in St Mark's gospel that after the resurrection Jesus appeared to two of his followers 'in another form . . . as they walked and went into the country' (16:12). The reference is clearly to the walk to Emmaus which Luke tells in detail (24:13–35). I would like to consider those words 'in another form' in a wider context.

One of the strange things about the post-resurrection appearances of Jesus – I think it is something we would not have suspected apart from revelation – is the different guises in which he revealed himself. To Cleopas and his companion on the Emmaus road he came simply as a fellow traveller, and it was only at the end of the day in the breaking of bread that his identity was revealed. To Mary, outside the tomb of the resurrection, he appeared as the gardener and was known only when he spoke her name. To the seven disciples, fishing off the shores of Galilee, he appeared on the beach once more as a stranger and was not recognised, at least not until the nets had been filled to breaking point with a huge quantity of fish. Even so we have the strange words that when they joined him no one dared ask him who he was, knowing it was the Lord. And it seems, too, from Luke's account (24:36–43) of our gospel story (Mark 16:9–20), telling of the appearance of Jesus in the upper room, that he was not at once recognised. Thus Luke tells us that the disciples were frightened, thinking that they had seen a ghost, and St John confirms Luke in saying that the first words of Jesus were a bestowal of peace, suggesting they were alarmed by this seeming stranger in their midst.

The disciples became convinced that it was indeed Jesus when he showed them the nail marks in his hands and his feet. Thomas, however, – who had not been with them (John 20:24) – remained an unbeliever, protesting that he would not believe until he had seen the marks for himself. The following week Jesus again appeared and Thomas was called out to examine the wounds. Perhaps it dawned on him then that Jesus was not only present

51

at that moment, but that he must have been present unseen when he had made his protest of disbelief out there in the market place or in the home or wherever it might have been. His confession 'My Lord and my God' goes beyond that of any of the other disciples.

It has always seemed to me strange that Jesus was not readily identifiable after the resurrection. Perhaps there is in this a sign that Jesus is always coming to us 'in another form'. We recall how St Francis of Assisi in the days leading up to his conversion dismounted from his horse to embrace a leper, and in him saw the face of Christ. Or how St Benedict taught his brothers that they were to receive one another and the guests to the monastery as Christ himself among them. In the well-known words of Albert Schweitzer, 'Christ comes to us as one unknown without a name, just as of old by the lakeside he came to those men who knew him not'. Yet for this truth we need not go beyond our Lord's own words: 'I was hungry and you fed me; naked and you clothed me; sick and you visited me . . . Inasmuch as you did it to one of these my little ones you did it unto me.' (Matthew 25:35, 36, 40).

We, too, are to find Christ in one another. People who come to us in Bede House often use expressions which convey the idea that they find Christ here. But let it be said that if any visitor finds Christ in us, it is the Christ in them which has seen the Christ in us, and so the Christ in them is available for us to recognise and feed on if we have not already done so. In so far as we become aware that every visitor is a bearer of Christ to us, to that degree shall we be able to bring Christ to them. Not that we shall be conscious of it, for it seems to be almost a law of the spiritual life that we give out most when we are least aware that we are giving out anything at all.

'Receive one another', says St Paul, 'as Christ Jesus received you.' And how does he receive us? – graciously, patiently and with a great compassion. Knowing how much we ourselves stand in need of the patience and compassion of Christ mediated through others, so too we are to be mediators of Christ to them. Thus we shall be Christ-bearers to one another, each finding in the other the agent of our deliverance.

~ 19 ~

Gluttony

> Brothers, be united in imitating me. Keep your eyes fixed on those
> who act according to the example you have from me. For there are
> so many people of whom I have often warned you, and now I warn
> you again with tears in my eyes, who behave like the enemies of
> Christ's cross. They are destined to be lost; their god is the stomach;
> they glory in what they should think shameful, since their minds
> are set on earthly things. But our homeland is in heaven and it is
> from there that we are expecting a Saviour, the Lord Jesus Christ,
> who will transfigure the wretched body of ours into the mould of
> his glorious body, through the working of the power which he has,
> even to bring all things under his mastery. (Philippians 3:17–21)

The words from the epistle 'whose God is their belly' lead me
to take gluttony as the subject of this address. However, let
me say by introduction that there are commentators who believe
that Paul's words are intended not to be taken solely in the sense
of over-eating, but in the wider sense suggested by the New
English Bible where the translation reads, 'appetite is their God'.
Ronald Knox, however, will have none of this and gives us the
translation, 'their own hungry bellies are the God they worship'.

Those of you who know John Macquarrie's *Dictionary of
Christian Ethics*[1] may have discovered the articles by Canon R. E.
C. Browne on the seven deadly sins. I have found all these articles
helpful but the one on gluttony struck me as being specially
valuable. It is short but is packed with suggestive material some
of which I would like to share with you.

The writer begins by speaking of the effects of over-eating –
something we must all have discovered to be true – that it dulls
the faculties, deadens general awareness, and makes concentration, thinking and prayer almost impossible. (Is it not strange
when in these days in which we realise as never before the
important role which the body has in prayer, we apply our insight

to posture and breathing and the like and so often fail to make the application to food?) The writer then goes on to make the important distinction between gluttony, which is simply 'the individual's failure to control a fleshly appetite', that is to say over-eating for the sheer enjoyment of the thing, what we would call greed – that on the one hand, and then on the other, what the writer of the article describes in these words:

> The gluttonous man, knowingly or unknowingly, uses food as others use drugs to give him pleasurable sensations which can help him for the time being to ignore the parts of his life which are boring, disturbing, or terrifying. Gluttony, like all sins of the flesh, must be considered spiritually. That is, whilst over-eating is a defect, the spiritual condition which permits it is very much more serious as it reveals the glutton's urgent need to escape reality.

There is a peculiarly modern ring about this approach, seeing over-eating as a means by which we operate, often unconsciously, an escape mechanism which brings temporary mental relief at the cost of evading a spiritual challenge. In modern parlance we know ourselves as compulsive eaters, usually an unhelpful label as it probably tends to reduce our resistance to self-control by suggesting we could do no other. Although plain greed may account for the excesses of most of us most of the time it may be doubted if any altogether escape the syndrome I have described. To recognise this may help to alert us to such occasions and so to be attentive to deal with them.

How is it we are to deal with them? I am thinking of us seculars (and largely so throughout this talk) who live in very different conditions from those in community. Merely to regulate at such times the amount of food taken – to do that and that alone – seems to me to do no more than to touch the surface of the problem. That is to deal with the symptom but to leave the cause untouched. We have to attend to the spiritual condition which lies behind. And that of course can never be the work of a moment. This sickness has become a part of us and we shall only find its healing in the whole round of living and working and praying. When anxieties or other forms of disturbance drive us to food, as another might be driven to alcohol or tobacco or some other drug, this may be the moment for taking one of those spaces we all need through the day, a few moments to realise that physical nourishment is our apparent but not our real need, our real need being to drop our anxieties in a renewed act of surrender to God. This then may be the moment for brief prayer, probably arid and difficult prayer, for if it were to be otherwise we would not be trying to evade it. I can only say what I find right for myself, though in all honesty I must add how often I fail. The root, then, is not in the realm of food, but in our spiritual need, and unnecessary indulgence in food is but one of the evasive devices.

Let me leave you, not with these thoughts, but with some heart-raising words from St Paul: 'Whatever you eat or drink do all for the glory of God . . . for everything is created by God and nothing is to be rejected if it is received with thanksgiving.'[2]

1. SCM, 1967.
2. Combining 1 Corinthians 10:31 and 1 Timothy 4:4.

∿ 20 ∿

The True Healing

The ten victims of skin-disease

Now it happened that on the way to Jerusalem he was travelling in the borderlands of Samaria and Galilee. As he entered one of the villages, ten men suffering from a virulent skin-disease came to meet him. They stood some way off and called to him, 'Jesus! Master! Take pity on us.' When he saw them he said, 'Go and show yourselves to the priests.' Now as they were going away they were cleansed. Finding himself cured, one of them turned back praising God at the top of his voice and threw himself prostrate at the feet of Jesus and thanked him. The man was a Samaritan. This led Jesus to say, 'Were not all ten made clean? The other nine, where are they? It seems that no one has come back to give praise to God, except this foreigner.' And he said to the man, 'Stand, up and go on your way. Your faith has saved you.' (Luke 17:11–19)

The story of the ten lepers in our gospel reading stands alone among the recorded healings of Jesus in that it was a group healing as distinct from a ministry to individuals. Standing afar off on account of the isolation imposed by their disease, they call as with one voice, 'Jesus, Master, have mercy on us'. The responding words, too, are spoken to them collectively: 'Go, show yourselves to the priests'. It was while on their way that their healing took place, whereupon one of them turned back praising God, and finding Jesus again, fell down before him giving thanks. Stress is laid on the fact that this man is a foreigner – the only one of the group – and for Luke this is no doubt supporting evidence that God has poured out his grace on the Gentiles also. For us today it can be a reminder that we are to place no limits, whether of Church or denomination or religion, on the extent of God's saving mercy.

The response of Jesus is variously translated in the modern versions of the New Testament. In most translations Jesus assures the man that his faith has cured him or made him well. This suggests that nothing has happened beyond the restoration of physical health. But the Greek suggests that more than that was intended. It seems to me that the Authorised Version comes closer to the truth in that it was 'wholth' rather than mere health which was bestowed upon this man. 'Thy faith has made thee whole.' Of modern versions the Jerusalem Bible alone supports the rendering with 'Your faith has saved you'. I think that the point which is being made is that whereas nine were cured (made well) only one was healed (made whole). It would certainly be in accordance with pastoral experience that the one to whom it was given to burst out in spontaneous praise and gratitude for his healing, and to acknowledge Jesus as its source, should be ready to receive a deeper gift than the others, who were simply restored to physical health. Far be it that we should under-rate the blessing of the physical health received by the nine who did not return. For them it meant a return to family and social relationships, the possibility of employment, the breaking down of isolation, and perhaps in time the overcoming of bitterness, self-pity and despair to which their disease might have exposed them.

But to this one man there belonged at this stage a deeper experience than the others, and for all of us it is 'wholth' and not health which is our deepest need: so it is that we ask God to give us what may best promote it. In most cases it will include present health, though there may be occasions where deprivation and sickness will for a while supply the outer circumstances which enable the Spirit to work at greater depth in our lives. We cannot say but it could be that this man was prepared through his sickness and isolation for the deliverance which is now his.

I have assumed that Luke means us to understand that this foreigner, this Samaritan, alone received a spiritual and not just a physical blessing, and further I have suggested that his capacity for praise and thanksgiving was in some way linked with the gift he had received. For it is surely in praise and thanksgiving that we become disposed to receive the richest gifts God has for us. Praise and gratitude, deep, generous and spontaneous, must surely be the least self-regarding and so the noblest emotion of which we are capable. In them we look away from the subjective concerns of self to an objective reality beyond. How insistent is St Paul, not simply that we should engage in the outward expression of praise but that its spirit should rule our lives: 'In everything give thanks for this is the will of God concerning you', or as the New English Bible translates, 'Give thanks whatever happens', that is to say not just when things go well but when they go badly too. And these are not just words, they are matched in Paul's life as, for example, when he glorifies God for his thorn in the flesh, a humiliating and painful affliction, and prays that God's strength may be made perfect in his weakness.

It is probable that when we thank and praise God for one another we enter into a deeper relationship than when we simply ask some blessing for them. Praise, whether directed towards God or our fellows, and especially where it has become the constant disposition of the heart, prepares us to receive the abundance of God's blessings. The point could be reinforced by considering how the opposite of thanksgiving – grumbling and discontent – are stunting to spiritual growth. They are accusations of God's want of goodness towards us, whereas praise is not only an acknowledgement of his providential ordering of our lives, but an opener of the heart which allows us to receive his grace in fuller measure. It is this to which every eucharist exposes us, as with angels and archangels and all the company of heaven we render to God our sacrifice of praise and thanksgiving.

The Victory of the Cross

Our theme today speaks of the victory of the cross. As I came to consider it, my mind was irresistibly taken to those massive words to be found in the prayer of consecration in the *Book of Common Prayer*: 'who made there (by his one oblation of himself once offered) a full, perfect, and sufficient sacrifice, oblation, and satisfaction, for the sins of the whole world'. I would not like to attempt to expound each word, but for me, as probably for most people, the sentence stands as a whole witnessing to the mighty act which was wrought upon the cross. The sentence challenges me to the recognition of God's holiness and to the reality of sin. It challenges me to see that Jesus was here dealing with a desperate situation, the situation caused by sin as the disturber of the order of the universe; that here was the meeting point between God's holiness and God's mercy, two aspects of his love, the first of which we too easily forget.

St Paul has many powerful metaphors in relationship to our Lord's death, but perhaps none so vivid as that in the epistle to the Colossians where he writes: 'Blotting out the handwriting of the ordinances which was against us, nailing it to the cross'. It is, I think, disappointing that both the Revised Standard Version and the New English Bible have changed the words 'blotting out the handwriting' to 'cancelling the bond', because this loses some of the force of Paul's metaphor.

Professor William Barclay points out that there is a Greek word (*chiazein*) which Paul might easily and naturally have used to signify the cancelling of a bond. The word begins with the Greek letter chi (ch pronounced as kh, as in khaki) which was made like our capital X. We put an X through a document to cancel it, but without realising that the letter stands for chi which in itself stood for *chiazein*, signifying the cancellation of the bond. But it seems, Barclay continues, that this is a word which Paul deliberately avoided, using a stronger word (*exaleiphein*) which means wiping out, as you would wipe out the sentences on a slate. This is a much more powerful metaphor than that of cancelling a bond. When you put a cross through a document you annul it but you can still read what was there. It is otherwise when you wipe a blackboard clean. 'It is as if God' (writes Barclay) 'in his amazing mercy, banished the record of our sins so completely that it was as if it had never been. It was gone in such a way that not a trace remained.' God does not scratch out an offending sentence. He reaches for the Tippex! Centuries before, the prophet Micah had offered an equally thorough-going image, speaking of God (7:19) being ready to cast Israel's sins into the depths of the sea. In those days, at least, there was an air of finality about that!

Here is the passage (Colossians 2:13–15) as J. B. Phillips translates it:

> You who were spiritually dead ... God has now made to share in the very life of Christ! He has forgiven you all your sins: Christ has utterly wiped out the damning evidence of broken laws and commandments which always hung over our heads, and has completely annulled it by nailing it over his head on the cross. And then, having drawn the sting of all the powers ranged against us, he exposed them, shattered, empty and defeated, in his final glorious and triumphant act!

'Christ was active (on the cross), resistant, on the offensive, not receiving blows but giving them, not having the floods go over him, but breasting them like a strong swimmer.'[1] And so at the end he could cry triumphantly in a loud voice, 'It is finished', words which we may spell out as: 'It is accomplished. I have completed the work you have given me to do.' That being the reality of Calvary, I almost think we need that massive rock-like sentence, 'full, perfect, and sufficient sacrifice, oblation, and satisfaction, for the sins of the whole world'. Even so, we must remember (with William Law)[2] that 'the precious blood of his Son was not poured out to pacify the Father (who in himself had no nature towards man but love), but it was poured out to quench the wrath and fire of the fallen soul, and to kindle in it a birth and light of love'.

60

1. Farmer, *The Healing Cross*.
2. Law believed, with Julian of Norwich, that God's love was pure compassion. With her, he saw the wrath to be, not in God but in us, waiting to be quenched by God's all-compassionate love.

∼ 22 ∼

The Comfortable Words

The good news revealed to the simple. The Father and the Son

At that time Jesus exclaimed, 'I bless you, Father, Lord of heaven and of earth, for hiding these things from the learned and the clever and revealing them to little children. Yes, Father, for that is what it pleased you to do. Everything has been entrusted to me by my Father; and no one knows the Son except the Father, just as no one knows the Father except the Son and those to whom the Son chooses to reveal him.

The gentle mastery of Christ

'Come to me, all you who labour and are overburdened, and I will give you rest. Shoulder my yoke and learn from me, for I am gentle and humble in heart, and you will find rest for your souls. Yes, my yoke is easy and my burden light.' (Matthew 11:25–30)

'Come unto me all that travail and are heavy laden and I will refresh you.' These words are doubly familiar for they reach us not only through the scriptures, as in the gospel passage, but, too, through the liturgy where they stand as the Comfortable Words. And, indeed, they have been comforting or strengthening – to get back to the root meaning of the word – to countless numbers, ourselves among them, reminding us that in our Saviour Christ the burden of sin is lifted and the waters of refreshment flow. They speak to us, too, in times of weariness or anxiety, bidding us to lay down our cares and worries, not to attempt to carry them in our own strength, but to abandon them into God's hands, casting all our care upon him, as the apostle Peter bids us do.

Yet it was in neither of these senses that the words were originally spoken, at least not primarily so. It was one of the contentions of Jesus against the Scribes and the Pharisees that 'they bind heavy burdens and grievous to be born and lay them on men's shoulders'. The weary and heavy laden were those who were bowed down by the burden of the law, often petty in its demands, circumscribing all the occasions of life, which the Pharisaic tradition had added to the great and broad principles of the law of Moses. It is, we may believe, not by accident that Matthew places these words just before the incident in the corn-fields on the Sabbath in which the disciples are accused of breaking the law by picking the ears of grain to satisfy their hunger. There follows immediately the story of the man with a withered hand healed by Jesus, again on the Sabbath. The Rabbis often referred to the law as a yoke and this same word is used of it in the New Testament. Peter, fighting for the liberty of the early Church at the Council of Jerusalem asks, 'Why do you make trial of God, by putting a yoke on the neck of the disciples which neither our fathers or we have been able to bear?'

The call to Christians is to freedom, the freedom of the lover in the presence of the beloved. In this freedom we are to grow. John the Baptist's words with reference to Jesus, 'He must increase, I must decrease' may also be understood metaphorically with reference to the old order and the new. Wise laws are needed to protect our growth in early days but as we put on Christ, law will fall into the background to become increasingly the one law of love. St Augustine is bold enough to bid us to love God and do what we like. In theory we can have no quarrel with that but in practice we know that such advice is apt to break down in times of stress and difficulty. Speaking for myself I am glad to have a framework of law in a place such as this which sets times for eucharist and offices, buttressing my own weakness. And this, it seems to me, is a help to putting on one's true freedom in Christ, which is not the freedom to do whatever one's human nature wants to do, but the freedom to be what God is calling one to be.

It is probably right to say that those who are members of religious communities know more than others of the freedom of love of which St Augustine speaks. But we are not to suppose that this freedom arises of necessity from a life undergirded by the rules which govern convent or monastic life. It would be possible to observe the Rule meticulously and yet to be greatly lacking in the love of God. The presence of law, especially where it extends to every part of daily life, presents a constant threat to one getting bogged down in a barren legalism whereby we fail to move on to the liberty to which we are called. There is indeed a constant tension between law and freedom, the freedom of those abandoned lovers of God whom we honour as saints. The task of every community is the delicate one of holding that tension in right balance.

Let us hold on to this paradox: law of its nature is binding and the purpose of law is to set free. For example, you have a rule (a law) to meet in this chapel on the dot seven times each day (if we include the night office at two in the morning). Nothing could be more binding than that. Often it must be most inconvenient to drop this or that task suddenly and make for the chapel. Yet what is the purpose of your life here? The purpose is not to garden or to cook or to read or to write, good and necessary as these things may be. But the over-riding purpose of your presence in community is to pray. And law has set you free to do just that. The rest will then find their rightful place as the overspill of prayer into daily life.

So long as law sets us free to be for God what he would have us be, it is good. When it no longer does that it has served its time and must be revised. May I leave you with the paradox: law of its nature is binding and the purpose of law is to set free.

∼ 23 ∼

Serving One Another

The washing of feet

Before the festival of the Passover, Jesus, knowing that his hour had come to pass from this world to the Father, having loved those who were his in the world, loved them to the end.

They were at supper, and the devil had already put it into the mind of Judas Iscariot son of Simon, to betray him. Jesus knew that the Father had put everything into his hands, and that he had come from God and was returning to God, and he got up from table, removed his outer garments and, taking a towel, wrapped it round his waist; he then poured water into a basin and began to wash the disciples' feet and to wipe them with the towel he was wearing.

He came to Simon Peter, who said to him, 'Lord, are you going to wash my feet?' Jesus answered, 'At the moment you do not know what I am doing, but later you will understand.' 'Never!' said Peter, 'You shall never wash my feet.' Jesus replied, 'If I do not wash you, you can have no share with me.' Simon Peter said, 'Well then, Lord, not only my feet, but my hands and my head as well!' Jesus said, 'No one who has had a bath needs washing, such a person is clean all over. You too are clean, though not all of you are.' He knew who was going to betray him, and that was why he said, 'though not all of you are'.

When he had washed their feet and put on his outer garments again he went back to the table. 'Do you understand', he said, 'what I have done to you? You call me Master and Lord, and rightly; so I am. If I, then, the Lord and Master, have washed your feet, you must wash each other's feet. I have given you an example so that you may copy what I have done to you.

'In all truth I tell you,
no servant is greater than his master,
no messenger is greater than the one who sent him.

'Now that you know this, blessed are you if you behave accordingly.'
(John 13:1–17)

65

St John's account of the washing of the disciples' feet, to which our gospel reading takes us, needs to be taken with the account of the last supper as given by St Luke. After the meal a dispute arose between the disciples as to which should be the greatest in the coming kingdom (Luke 22:24–27). Jesus replied that it was not to be with his followers as it was with worldly princes, but rather that the greatest would be as the least, and the leader as one who served. Jesus continues: 'Which is the greater, the one who sits at table or the one who serves? Is it not the one who sits at table? But I am among you as one who serves.' This seems to set the scene for the foot-washing, though Luke himself gives no account of the event.

Jesus, John tells us, rises from supper, lays aside his outer garments, takes a basin and wraps himself round with a towel, stoops and washes the feet of these men whom he loves. It must have been an example for them – as it is for us – for the rest of their lives. Yet I find it hard to believe it was done as an example. What we do as Christians often stands as an example but that we should do it as an example is at least questionable. Parents who go to church regularly set their children a good example, but if they go for that reason their churchgoing is unlikely to have the effect they intend. Actions which stand as an example will be those done in purity of intention without sideways glances at how others may regard them. It seems to me that the clue to the foot-washing is given in the first verse of our gospel passage: 'having loved his own that were in the world, he loved them to the end'. Here was a spontaneous act of love for these twelve men – its form being determined by the conversation recorded by Luke – with whom he had shared the past three years (and Judas was still among them), the joys and hardships, the times of growth and deepening insight, the times, too, of failure and disappointment. Jesus loved them and accepted them into his friendship as they were, just as he accepts and loves us as we are. Of one thing there could be no doubt – their loyalty, or at least their desire to be loyal. Thomas had spoken for them all when he had said, 'Let us go to Jerusalem that we may die with him'.

We do not know the order in which the foot-washing took place. But at least it appears that Peter was some way down the line. He was not therefore taken by surprise. He had time to determine what his reaction would be. It could be that in protesting he came out better than the others. There may have been a silent protest in the hearts of all and perhaps Peter alone had the courage to speak. 'Lord, do you wash my feet? You shall never wash my feet.' At least the reply had application to them all. 'If I do not wash you, you have no part in me.' If after these three years you are still unable to understand that the mark of a disciple is the way of lowly service then you are certainly not ready to be one of mine. Peter's reply fits in with all that we know of his character: 'Lord, not my feet only, but my hands and my head'.

We all have to learn, as did Peter, to accept the service of others and to some natures that is not easy. There are many who can give generously and yet when it comes to receiving their weakness is exposed. The reason is not hard to see. When we give to another we put that person (unconsciously no doubt) into our debt, and if this does not actively minister to our pride, at least it makes no demand on humility. But when we accept a service from others we become indebted to them, and to respond graciously calls for a deeper humility than when we ourselves are the giver, which may call for none at all.

It may perhaps be asked how this fits in with the saying of Jesus recorded in the Acts of the Apostles (20:35) that it is more blessed to give than to receive. I think we have to understand that there may be occasions when receiving is the deepest form of giving. If we decline an offer of help we are denying the other the pleasure of helping us, and so it follows that in accepting their offer, whilst we are in one sense receiving, in a deeper sense we are giving. Nowadays young people don't very much offer their seats to the elderly on bus or train, but where that is done it is gracious to accept it.

Our salvation begins with a great acceptance. The very first blow of the salvation experience is directed towards our pride. 'By grace are you saved through faith, not of works lest anyone should boast.' Our love is a response. As we become increasingly open to receive God's love so does our own love grow. Every eucharist is a reminder, and especially as we approach the altar rails, that God has acted first, and that we are dependent upon him for our well-being at every level.

24

The Holy Name of Jesus

Joseph adopts Jesus as his son

This is how Jesus Christ came to be born. His mother Mary was betrothed to Joseph; but before they came to live together she was found to be with child through the Holy Spirit. Her husband Joseph, being an upright man and wanting to spare her disgrace, decided to divorce her informally. He had made up his mind to do this when suddenly the angel of the Lord appeared to him in a dream and said, 'Joseph son of David, do not be afraid to take Mary home as your wife, because she has conceived what is in her by the Holy Spirit. She will give birth to a son and you must name him Jesus, because he is the one who is to save his people from their sins. Now all this took place to fulfil what the Lord had spoken through the prophet:

> Look! the virgin is with child and will give birth to a son
> whom they will call Immanuel,

a name which means 'God-is-with-us'. When Joseph woke up he did what the angel of the Lord had told him to do: he took his wife to his home; he had not had intercourse with her when she gave birth to a son; and he named him Jesus. (Matthew 1:18–25)

'Thou shalt call his name Jesus for he shall save his people from their sins' (1:21). These words are from the Gospel for the Feast of the Holy Name. Names, as we know, were very important to people of biblical times and for the Jews they generally had religious significance. A name would be changed to mark a crisis in a person's life, a new commission laid upon them by God. So Abram became Abraham, and Jacob became Israel, and Saul became Paul. Jesus, too, would mark character by a special name. Thus Simon was called Peter or Rock man (Rocky, as we might say today) and James and John became Boanerges or Sons of Thunder.

One of the Old Testament characters to be given a new name was Joshua. He had been known as Oshea, but as leader of God's people he was to become Joshua, meaning 'He whose salvation is Yahweh'. The name Jesus is of the same derivation as Joshua and means 'God's salvation'. In our Lord's time it was quite a common name but later the Jews avoided it because of their dislike for Christianity and Christians avoided it for reasons of reverence. For them this was the name above every name. 'Jesus, for thy name's sake,' said St Augustine, 'do that for me which thy name proclaims. Name of delight, name of comfort to sinners, name of blessed hope. For what does thy name Jesus mean but saviour. Therefore, for thy name's sake, be to me Jesus a merciful Saviour.'

'Thou shalt call his name Jesus for he shall save his people from their sins.' Salvation is viewed in the Bible broadly in three ways. It is something which has taken place in the past. It is a continuing process in the present. And it is to be completed in the future. If Christians remembered these three aspects of salvation it would help to clear up misunderstandings between various groups. The 'brother, are-you-saved?' type of Christian appears to think of salvation largely in terms of a past experience. At the other end of the Christian spectrum the merit-conscious person seems to think of it in terms of the future. The biblical picture is one of balance, holding together the three aspects of salvation. When Paul writes to the Ephesians he speaks of salvation as something already achieved: 'by grace you have been saved through faith' (Ephesians 2:8). But we are not to rest in an experience of the past. That would be to make a moral identification with those Jews who counted on salvation in virtue of their descent from Abraham.

But Paul sees salvation, too, as a continuing process. 'You must work out your own salvation,' Paul writes to the Philippians 'in fear and trembling for it is God who works in you inspiring both the will and the deed' (Philippians 2:12). Every day, every hour, every moment is the moment of salvation. It is easier to trust in an experience of the past than to correspond faithfully, moment by moment, with the impulse of the Spirit in the present.

And then salvation is seen as something to be realised in the future, as when Paul writes to the Thessalonians that God has *destined* us for the full attainment of salvation through Jesus Christ

(1 Thessalonians 5:9). Jesus, too, says that he who holds out to the end *will* be saved (Matthew 10:22). Patience, endurance, courage are qualities we shall need till the end. Finally, there is one saying from St Paul, made familiar through the epistle for Advent Sunday, where past, present and future are brought together in a single verse. 'Now [indicating the present] is our salvation nearer [indicating an end] than when we first believed [indicating a beginning]' (Romans 13:11).

We may gather these thoughts together in a simple illustration. A swimmer is in difficulty and is in danger of drowning. As he sees someone dive from the bank hope begins to dawn. As his rescuer firmly grasps him he calls out, 'I'm saved'. There is reason and truth in this exclamation but clearly he is not saved yet. He is bidden to lie on his back while his rescuer tows him to the bank. He co-operates all he can. Once more, as he is being towed to the shore, he calls out with relief, 'I'm saved'. True, and yet not true, for he is only in the process of being saved. As the two reach the bank willing hands pull him from the water. Again he calls out, 'I'm saved', and this of course represents the consummation of the process of salvation which lies beyond the experience of death. It is such a simple illustration that I hardly dare tell it to you! The rescuer is, of course, Jesus, who humbled himself for us and our salvation. And we may with truth say that we are saved at every moment of the saving experience because so long as we commit ourselves into the hands of Christ our saviour, he will surely bring to completion the good work he has begun. For, with Paul, we are persuaded that neither death nor life, nor principalities nor powers, nor things present nor things to come, nor any other creature shall be able to separate us from the love of God which is in Christ Jesus our Lord.

25

The Freedom of the Sons of God

> But now that faith has come we are no longer under a slave looking
> after us; for all of you are the children of God, through faith, in
> Christ Jesus, since every one of you that has been baptised has been
> clothed in Christ. There can be neither Jew nor Greek, there can be
> neither slave nor freeman, there can be neither male nor female –
> for you are all one in Christ Jesus. (Galatians 3:25–28)

The theme of this part of the Epistle to the Galatians (3:25–4:7)
is the freedom of the sons of God. St Paul tells us that for
those who have put on Christ 'there is neither Jew nor Greek,
slave nor free, male nor female, for you are all one in Christ
Jesus' (3:28). Again, in the same letter (5:1) Paul writes: 'Freedom
is what we have – Christ has set us free! Stand, then, as free
people, and do not allow yourselves to become slaves again.'

Paul works out his theme with special reference to the question
of circumcision around which controversy centred in his time.
Some Christians held that all Gentile converts must submit to
this rite as Jewish converts had already done in requirement of
the Jewish law. Others, however, were more liberal and they saw
clearly, as did Paul himself, that what mattered was (in the words
of our collect) 'the true circumcision of the spirit, that our hearts
and all our members being mortified from all worldly and carnal
lusts, we may, in all things obey thy blessed will'.

In the time of Jesus the literal adherence to the law – the
obedience to the letter rather than to the spirit – made its impact
upon him chiefly in relation to the keeping of the Sabbath. His
disciples were criticised for eating the ears of corn as they walked
through the fields on the Sabbath day, and he was on several
occasions taken to task for healing on the Sabbath. The fourth
commandment, which related to the Sabbath, instead of giving
men and women an opportunity for recreation and worship and
rest, had become hedged around with petty and tyrannical laws,

71

reducing them to the status of slaves. They were slaves to law, unable on this of all days to experience their freedom as children of God. Christ gave the great charter of freedom: 'the Sabbath was made for man, not man for the Sabbath'.

And so St Paul tells us to stand fast in the liberty which is ours in Christ. All Christians in a measure know and experience the liberty of the sons of God. And yet our liberty is not as it shall be. We grow, as we respond to grace, into an ever-deepening experience of it. Wherever we are bound to law in a narrow or legalistic way we are, in a strict sense, guilty of idolatry for we are entertaining a false conception of God. So it was with many of the Pharisees. Their frenzied and scrupulous concern for the law blinded them to a vision of God as a loving Father. Instead he became a hard taskmaster exacting the last drop of sweat from his children. Such a distorted vision constitutes idolatry.

But we do not have to look to a distant past to see this principle at work. We may well find pockets in our own lives where we cannot enter into the freedom of the Spirit though we know quite well in our heads that in God's sight such freedom may be ours. In such cases we must exercise patience and love, whether with others or with ourselves. The time will come when the 'feeling' side of our nature will allow us to do what is beyond us now. Where the scruple affects another, Paul tells us that love is to be at all times supreme and that it may be right to restrict our own liberty when it becomes a cause of offence. 'If food is a cause of my brother falling, I will never eat meat lest I cause my brother to fall.'

It is usually fear which keeps us restricted in the limiting ways in which we have been brought up. And it is love which releases us into our freedom. As St John tells us, it is perfect love which casts out fear. As our love grows in perfection so, too, will grow our liberty in Christ. Even so we shall need the help of wise law for a long while yet. St Augustine's 'Love God, and do what you like', whilst excellent in principle, may easily become a cause of self-deception. Some rules there must be, as everyone in a religious community must know so well, but always we are to remember that they are there to set us free, not free to do whatever our impulsive natures urge us to do, but free to be the sort of person God would have us to be, and to respond to the way of life he intends for us.

⁓ 26 ⁓

The Peace of God

> As the chosen of God, then, the holy people whom he loves, you are to be clothed in heartfelt compassion, in generosity and humility, gentleness and patience. Bear with one another; forgive each other if one of you has a complaint against another. The Lord has forgiven you; now you must do the same. Over all these clothes, put on love, the perfect bond. And may the peace of Christ reign in your hearts, because it is for this that you were called together in one body. Always be thankful.
>
> Let the Word of Christ, in all its richness, find a home with you. Teach each other, and advise each other, in all wisdom. With gratitude in your hearts sing psalms and hymns and inspired songs to God; and whatever you say or do, let it be in the name of the Lord Jesus, in thanksgiving to God the Father through him. (Colossians 3:12–17)

From our epistle I take these words: 'Let the peace of God rule in your hearts' (3:15). It comes as a surprise to many that the New Testament gives us little encouragement to search for peace. There is in fact only one passage telling us to seek peace, and it comes in the first epistle of St Peter: 'He who would love life and see good days, let him seek peace and pursue it'. These are, however, not Peter's own words but are a quotation from Psalm 34. Speaking generally, we could say of New Testament teaching that peace is a quality which steals into a person's life, almost unnoticeably, as a consequence of a right relationship with God. It is, as it were, the by-product of something beyond itself. Thus Jesus does not bid us to seek for peace, but rather that we may come to know the things which belong to our peace. Seek the peace of God and you may miss it. Seek the God of peace and you will find God and the peace which necessarily follows.

We cannot separate this verse from what has gone before. Earlier in our epistle Paul refers to Jesus as the image of the invisible God, the first born of all creation in whom all things hold together, reconciling us to himself, making peace by the blood of the cross. 'He is our peace' says Paul, breaking down the partition between ourselves and God, the barrier erected by the rebelliousness of sin. Paul sees the cross as an event of cosmic significance, effecting on a world scale what we could never achieve for ourselves, the place where the contradiction was resolved between God's holiness and our sin. And the peace of God, which is to be one of the distinguishing marks of the Christian life, is to be seen not as the result of our striving, but as flowing from our acceptance in faith of Christ's saving work and our assurance of God's continued graciousness towards us. This is a peace which may be experienced with special emotional intensity at particular times such as, for example, at the moment of conversion, or after one's first confession, but it would be wrong to measure the depth of peace in our lives by our sensible feelings.

As we grow in Christ peace is deepened within us, but this comes about by the breaking up of a partly false peace, usually through suffering – pain of body, bereavement, temptation, humiliation – making room for a deeper peace to take its place. During this period it may seem that the peace we had once known has left us, but that is not so for peace can continue in the depths of the soul even though the senses are involuntarily disturbed – just as the ocean remains calm in the depths whilst the surface is ruffled by the wind. It may not be clear at the time how this can be but it becomes clear afterwards, for when the trial has passed we find that we have emerged purified and strengthened, with peace more firmly established, and less dependent on the external vicissitudes of life.

'Seek peace and pursue it' says St Peter, quoting from the psalms but that, as we have seen, is a sentiment standing on its own in the New Testament, and in any case it probably had a social rather than a personal emphasis. Rather than to advise anyone to seek peace it would be wiser to invite them to enter into the peace which is already theirs in Christ, to renew their faith and hope in him. 'Let go' (we might say to another or to ourselves) 'of those vain fears which spring from the devil or your disordered imagination. Let go. Don't cling. Hold fast to your Lord. The victory is won. Enter into its fruits.' This may not be easy but it has psychological as well as theological justification. It makes a vast difference to your approach whether you are searching for a house or engaged in occupying a house which is already there.

The seeking of the God of peace rather than the peace of God has a thoroughly scriptural ring. 'O God, thou art my God, early will I seek thee.' 'Like as the hart desireth the water brooks so longeth my soul after thee, O God.' The psalms are full of such aspirations. All Christian prayer, whether it be in the form of meditation upon some theme leading to the forming of resolutions, as is usual in the early stages of the Christian life, or whether it be the aspirative prayer of the Offices, or the silent imageless prayer made familiar in *The Cloud of Unknowing*, is, if integrated with life as a whole, a seeking and finding of God. And especially we may say this of the last form of prayer, with the intent of the will towards God in the nakedness of faith, with memory and imagination stilled. For here the Holy Spirit is seeking to reach down to the depths of our beings. Our faults and failures are due in no small measure to disharmony at the centre. When the Holy Spirit cleanses us here his healing spreads to every part of our lives. All such prayer is an entering into peace because it is in the first place an entering into God.

27

The More Excellent Way

Though I command languages both human and angelic – if I speak without love, I am no more than a gong booming or a cymbal clashing. And though I have the power of prophecy, to penetrate all mysteries and knowledge, and though I have all the faith necessary to move mountains – if I am without love, I am nothing. Though I should give away to the poor all that I possess, and even give up my body to be burned – if I am without love, it will do me no good whatever.

Love is always patient and kind; love is never jealous; love is not boastful or conceited, it is never rude and never seeks its own advantage, it does not take offence or store up grievances. Love does not rejoice at wrongdoing, but finds its joy in the truth. It is always ready to make allowances, to trust, to hope and to endure whatever comes.

Love never comes to an end. But if there are prophecies, they will be done away with; if tongues, they will fall silent; and if knowledge, it will be done away with. For we know only imperfectly, and we prophesy imperfectly; but once perfection comes, all imperfect things will be done away with. When I was a child, I used to talk like a child, and see things as a child does, and think like a child; but now that I have become an adult, I have finished with all childish ways. Now we see only reflections in a mirror, mere riddles, but then we shall be seeing face to face. Now, I can know only imperfectly; but then I shall know just as fully as I am myself known.

As it is, these remain: faith, hope and love, the three of them; and the greatest of them is love. (1 Corinthians 13)

Today's theme, 'the more excellent way', takes us to one of the best-known and best-loved passages in the New Testament. The passage in 1 Corinthians 13 falls into three natural divisions. The first tells that the most costly sacrifices are valueless without love. The second describes the various excellencies of love. And the third tells of the imperishable nature of love. And yet love does not stand alone, 'there abideth these three, faith, hope and love'. This is not an accidental association. The three stand together. There is an organic relationship between them. Our hymn for Lauds on Friday reminded us:

> The *faith* that first must be possessed,
> Root deep within our inmost breast;
> And joyous *hope* in second place,
> Then *charity* thy greatest grace.

Our English language is often less subtle in shades of meaning than the Greek in which the New Testament was written. It is common knowledge that the word 'love' in English has to do duty for several words in the Greek. There is *eros* which stands for passionate or sexual love, from which we get our word 'erotic'. There is *storge* which is linked especially with family affection. There is *philia* which is especially related to friendship. And there is *agape*, the word used in this passage, which has to do primarily with the will and not the emotions. The person who looks upon another with unconquerable good will, whether that person be likeable or unlikeable, or whether they be friend or foe, this person is showing *agape* to his neighbour.

Faith, hope and *agape* stand together in the passage before us, as they must always do on this side of death. If *agape* lacked the theological dimension supplied by faith and hope it would fail to see the person to whom it was directed as a child of God with a destiny beyond this world, and would thus have a temporal rather than an eternal perspective. Such an *agape* would, for example, find it kinder to all concerned to prevent handicapped children from coming to birth. And why should the elderly, it would ask, live on in weakness and discomfort when an injection would take them back into the nothingness from which they came? A humanistic love may be costly to the one who offers it, but if it is wrongly directed it may do much harm. The extravagant presents which parents give their children might be cited as a humanist *agape* which probably spoils rather than helps those who receive them.

It is very different where *agape* is linked with faith and hope. By faith Paul means a total trust and commitment to God as revealed in Jesus. In every life there will be times of crisis and these are the special testing times of faith. At such times faith means holding on in the midst of obscurity and bewilderment and distress to what in our rational moments we know to be true. All must pass through this crucible of suffering for it is in the testing of faith that it is made strong. Our choice as Christians is not whether we suffer or whether we do not, but rather whether, given suffering, it shall be fruitful and expanding or stunting and dwarfing. 'There is only one way to live,' it has been said, 'and that is to die daily.'

Hope is closely related to faith. Its importance can, perhaps, best be appreciated by considering its opposite, which is despair. Despair, to throw up everything, to give up attempting to go on, is the final tragedy of life. Hope is the confidence that God who has already begun a good work in ourselves or others will bring it to completion in the day of Christ. Hope is faith projected into the future, and it is founded on faith in the great acts of our redemption wrought for us in the past. Perhaps we give too little thought to the theological virtue of hope. We need to make acts of hope especially in times of defeat and failure. Christian hope is as far removed from ordinary optimism as Christian love (*agape*) is from human benevolence.

And so we come back to love. In the passage before us Paul outlines its range and dimension; its patience and goodness; its humility and hiddenness and tenderness; its generosity and freedom from self-seeking; its perseverance and endurance; but all, be it remembered, in the setting of faith and hope. This *agape* is the quality of God's own life, constant, faithful and enduring, ever seeking to enable us to break through to new levels of truth and reality, yet patient and compassionate, content to wait lest we be overwhelmed. And now abideth these three, faith, hope and love, but the greatest of these is love.

∼ 28 ∼

Meekness

Our epistle (Galatians 5:13–25) brings before us the fruits of the Spirit, and I would like to speak of the eighth of these: meekness. Meekness is a strong and noble virtue which is unhappily often associated in people's minds with an insipid, milk-and-water quality of life, the antithesis of virility and strength.

Professor Barclay in his New Testament Word Book tells us that the Greek word *praus* which is translated 'meek' is a lovely word standing for gentle when used of things, such as a gentle wind or a gentle voice, and for mild or gracious when used of persons. So far it would fit in with the general modern biblical rendering of gentleness. But Barclay goes on to give two other shades of meaning of *praus* which give meekness its own special distinctive quality. He says that Aristotle regarded *praus* as the mean between two extremes, the extremes of anger and (to use Barclay's word) angerlessness. Seen in this light the meek Christian is like his master in that he has the capacity for anger when the occasion demands it, when he is, let us say, in the presence of ruthless and defiant evil, directed not against himself but against another whom he feels bound to defend. The meek man alone is then able to fulfil that most difficult of all apostolic commands: to be angry and not to sin. This is because his indignation is free from petulance or touchiness or wounded pride. No doubt this response is to be exercised sparingly and, when evil is directed against himself, the meek man will respond in patience, gentleness and self-control, committing himself and his adversary into God's hands, overcoming evil with good, standing firm in the invincibility of love. Such was the way of Jesus in his Passion.

I think there are many who would hold anger to be never justified and would say that a part of what I have said has no place in Christian character. Yet the world would surely be a place of less nobility without its John the Baptists and Trevor Huddlestones. But let it be stressed that it is only meekness which can preserve anger as a moral and purifying force. Separated from meekness, anger is destructive and soul-destroying, a snare for those who exercise it, and for its victims, not only barren and unproductive, but a source of misery and wretchedness.

Barclay gives one more thought about the meaning of this word *praus*. It was used for the wild animal which had been tamed, and so meekness, far from being feebleness and want of spirit, is to be seen as strength under control. The horse, once wild and unrestrained, is now obedient to bit and bridle.

How well this fits in with one of the greatest figures of the Old Testament, of whom it was written: 'Now Moses was the meekest man on the face of the earth.' The life of Moses, if we follow St Stephen's speech in the Acts of the Apostles, was divided into three forty-year periods. At the end of the first period when he was a passionate and impulsive young man, uncontrolled anger so surged within him that he murdered one of Pharaoh's overseers whom he saw ill-treating a fellow Jew. There followed a long period away from Egypt whilst God was preparing him for his life work. This was the time of breaking in, of the curbing and taming of natural and uncontrolled impulse, the fashioning of character, disciplined, obedient and restrained. Then only was he a fit instrument for God's purpose. It is true that the fire remained and at times burst into flame, but we now have a balancing picture which gives us the assurance of the purity of that flame. We follow Moses into the wilderness and hear him plead with God, 'Oh these people have sinned a great sin and have made them gods of gold. Yet now if thou wilt forgive their sin . . . and if not, blot *me*, I pray thee, out of the book which thou hast written'. It was this combination of an ardent and flaming spirit with a fatherly tenderness and concern for his people, which earned Moses the right to be called meek above all others of his time. This much misunderstood virtue depending, as it does, on faith and courage in heroic measure is one of the most attractive and compelling of the fruits of the Spirit. Gentleness will be its normal manifestation, but gentleness born of strength and not of weakness.

In the case of an erring brother, says St Paul, he is to be restored 'in a spirit of meekness lest you also be tempted', showing meekness to be the very opposite of self-righteousness, the sin which above all others is our death warrant and condemnation. The people of Ephesus are told that meekness with lowliness and patience is the very bond of peace, and Paul tells the Church at Corinth to wear meekness as a part of its daily dress. And when Jesus bids all who are burdened, jaded and strained to find in him that repose which will bring with it a new strength, it is the qualities of meekness and lowliness which he uses to give his appeal its drawing and compelling power.

'Thou must be meeked', says *The Cloud of Unknowing* in its quaint medieval English. Yes indeed, for we cannot 'meek' ourselves. Only the Holy Spirit can do that as we allow ourselves to be pliable in God's hands, accepting trustfully all that he shall ordain whether by way of comfort or trial – in Peter's words, entrusting our souls to him as a faithful creator.

29

Miracle at Cana

The wedding at Cana

On the third day there was a wedding at Cana in Galilee. The mother of Jesus was there, and Jesus and his disciples had also been invited. And they ran out of wine, since the wine provided for the feast had all been used, and the mother of Jesus said to him, 'They have no wine.' Jesus said, 'Woman, what do you want from me? My hour has not come yet.' His mother said to the servants, 'Do whatever he tells you.' There were six stone water jars standing there, meant for the ablutions that are customary among the Jews: each could hold twenty or thirty gallons. Jesus said to the servants, 'Fill the jars with water,' and they filled them to the brim. Then he said to them, 'Draw some out now and take it to the president of the feast.' They did this; the president tasted the water, and it had turned into wine. Having no idea where it came from – though the servants who had drawn the water knew – the president of the feast called the bridegroom and said, 'Everyone serves good wine first and the worse wine when the guests are well wined; but you have kept the best wine till now.'

This was the first of Jesus' signs: it was at Cana in Galilee. He revealed his glory, and his disciples believed in him. After this he went down to Capernaum with his mother and his brothers and his disciples, but they stayed there only a few days. (John 2:1–12)

The changing of the water into wine at Cana is the first of the signs in St John's gospel. St John refers to all the miracles of his gospel as signs. There is a sense in which every miracle is a sign, a sign that the kingdom of God has come with power and a sign of God's compassion revealed in Jesus. But the miracles of John's gospel are usually taken to be signs in a more special sense. They are chosen to point to some particular teaching about Jesus' mission and person.

The presence of Jesus at a wedding is a sign that he came to sanctify all life, to lift up the commonplace that it may be known to be the place of God's dealing with us. Here we see him as the Lord of joys and recreation. All the actions of Jesus are in one way or another a revelation of the kingdom which is ushered in with his ministry. In this sign the revelation is related to every part of our life. The everyday occupations, the business and pleasures of ordinary people, marriage – the most vital relationship – these do not lie outside his kingdom but are a part of it, to be developed and enriched by the sanctifying action of the Holy Spirit. The sign should help us to see life as a whole, to beware of making false divisions between the 'religious' and the 'secular', but to see our dedication as extending to everything in which we are caught up.

The wine had failed, and it is this failure which gave Jesus the opportunity for his creative work. God's action is always in relationship to our need. The coming to an end of our natural gifts is the occasion of God's opportunity. We may take comfort in this. The poorer we are in natural gifts the more we may look to him to fulfill our needs. Not many wise after the flesh, not many mighty, not many noble are called, but God has chosen the foolish things to confound the wise, the weak things to confound the mighty. Being aware that our calling makes demands upon us beyond our human capacity to meet them, we must take to heart St Paul's words: 'Most gladly will I glory in my weakness that the power of God may rest upon me.'

'They have no wine.' It is more than a statement, these words of Mary. It is a prayer, because there is a note of expectancy. Yet it is a prayer of deep humility. The need is stated and nothing more. There is no presuming to determine how the prayer shall be answered. It is likely that as we grow in the Spirit our prayers will more and more conform to this pattern.

And then our Lord's reply. 'Mother, you must let me respond here in my own way. My time for action has not yet come.' But Mary, knowing that her son meant to do something to meet the need, turns to the servants and tells them to do what he says. And what is it he tells them? Something quite inadequate. 'Fill the pots with water.' But, though inadequate, it had to be done. How like this is to our own lives! To change the imagery for a moment, all that we do can be likened to dry bones waiting to be clothed by the Spirit. We say our offices. What are they but mere words, unless they are breathed upon by the Spirit? Yet we must say them. We must present these dry bones before the Lord, waiting for him to clothe them. We give our talks, if that is our calling, but of what value are they unless they take life from the indwelling Spirit? We say our prayers. We go apart. We are silent. We are still. But what of it all? This is but a filling of the jars with water, of no ultimate value in itself, but this, what we can do, has to be done in preparation for the Lord's action. It is the same for the artist, the craftsman, the writer, the musician. They must betake themselves to the tools of their trade and, doing what is within their power, wait for the breathing of the Spirit.

The gospel passage tells us that the servants filled the jars to the brim. Here is a reminder that we have to do our utmost. Yet when we have done all, apart from him, we have done nothing. The water awaits the touch of his creative hand. 'Pour out now.' It seems natural to believe that the water became wine in the pouring. We may reflect on how often it is in the act of doing something that the strength is given. The inspiration is given not in advance but as we work, as we prepare or give this talk, as we say this office or write this letter.

The wine was pronounced good but its origin remained unknown. Once again, how true to life! People who come to this place often remark on the love and joy which they find here. Yet not all know where it comes from, that it originates in your offices and prayers. The contemplative life, seen by some to be a waste of time, has a healing power beyond all other. We don't have to speak of it to visitors any more than Jesus had to explain himself to the ruler of the feast. It is enough that they experience the fruits. The fuller revelation may be awaited.

30

The Works of the Devil

Our collect today speaks of the works of the devil.

> O God, whose blessed Son was manifested that he might destroy the works of the devil, and make us the sons of God, and heirs of eternal life: Grant us, we beseech thee, that, having this hope, we may purify ourselves, even as he is pure; that, when he shall appear again with power and great glory, we may be made like unto him in his eternal and glorious kingdom . . .

What are the works of the devil? St John's gospel tells us that when Jesus speaks to the Pharisees of the devil he describes him as a liar and as the father of lies. But there is an even more serious charge than that. 'There is no truth in him', and 'When he speaks he speaks according to his own nature'. And this is our Lord's basic condemnation of the Pharisee, that being blinded by pride he had become a lie, thus making false all that he said or did. The Pharisees were not conscious liars. If by lying we mean speaking in such a way that our words do not correspond with what we believe to be true then, in that sense, the Pharisees were not lying when they said to Jesus, 'Now we know you have a demon'. It was worse than that. Having become a lie (which is further down the moral scale than becoming a liar) they truly believed what they said. If the Pharisees had been liars, pure and simple, they would have known themselves to be so and repentance would have been open to them. But it must be otherwise when deceit entwines the roots of personality. Without awareness of falsehood the Pharisees were able to say, 'We see'. And, as Jesus said to them, 'it is because you say "we see" that your guilt remains'.[1]

What I have said of the Pharisees who opposed Jesus (no doubt with exaggeration in order the better to make the point), Jesus himself said of the devil. The root accusation against the devil is not that he consciously deceives, but that having become a lie he propagates error and falsehood out of his own inner deception, this being united to his odious nature as a foul stench is to a load of manure. To say this goes beyond, but does not exclude, conscious fraud and deceit, which is one of Satan's most menacing and intimidating weapons.

If what I have said is true then it follows that the most absolute enemies of society are not the frauds and cheats who, in the process of deceiving, are aware of their deception, but rather those whose godlessness and pride has so blinded their minds that they propagate falsehood and lies in the inner conviction that they are disseminating truth. Most people will have no problem in believing Lenin and Stalin were not liars in promoting their system. It was worse than that. They had, in Paul's expressive phrase, exchanged the truth of God for a lie. They were not so much liars as, in their godlessness, become blinded to the truth.

When Paul spoke of those who had exchanged the truth of God for a lie he was speaking of the sins of the flesh. Here, too, we see the devil at work today. Those who believe, and try to make others believe, that there is something progressive and desirable about a society in which promiscuity of every sort – disobedience, greed and moral lawlessness – are to be pursued as good, are probably not being insincere so far as their own inner consciousness is concerned, but have rather become (or are becoming) blinded to the truth. In spite of so much around us which is lovely and of good report, I believe we have a satanic influence, fearful and horrifying, gnawing at the heart of our national life.

But what of us within the Church? Is it that we have no blind spots? Do we forget that our arguments started from our Lord's confrontation with the Pharisees, the religious leaders of their day? There was no automatic safeguard in their day in being children of Abraham, and there is none in ours in being baptised or holding responsibility in the Church. We shall be judged, as they were judged, by our acceptance or rejection of Jesus, his standards, his values, his qualities of love and care and concern.

Jesus was manifested, our collect tells us, that he might destroy the works of the devil, and he does this by being the light which dispels the darkness, the good which overcomes evil and the truth which reveals error. Jesus comes among us as the way, the truth and the life. The battle is now joined and will continue until all things are gathered together in him. Our hope in Jesus is, as the collect says, the condition of our purification, and in turn our purification marks the measure in which we have entered into the truth of Jesus, and so are effective instruments in the warfare against evil.

And so to the last phrase, in which we ask that we may be made like unto Jesus in his eternal and glorious kingdom. The words are a reminder of the words of the epistle (1 John 3:1–8): 'We know that, when he shall appear, we shall be like him; for we shall see him as he is.' What a wonderful thing it will be to see him as he is! Yes, indeed, if we are like him, but if not, the vision, if granted, would be unbearable. We become like him as God reveals to us, not merely the poverty, but the hopelessness of our state in so far as we are not caught up in his saving work. As we cast ourselves upon the mercy of Christ our Saviour, he purifies us even as he is pure, and prepares us for the vision of himself. To which we pray he will bring us all. Amen.

1. The conflict of Jesus with the Pharisees is largely found in chapters 5 to 11 of St John's Gospel.

∿ 31 ∿

Justification by Faith

Faith guarantees salvation

So then, now that we have been justified by faith, we are at peace with God through our Lord Jesus Christ; it is through him, by faith, that we have been admitted into God's favour in which we are living, and look forward exultantly to God's glory. Not only that; let us exult, too, in our hardships, understanding that hardship develops perseverance, and perseverance develops a tested character, something that gives us hope, and a hope which will not let us down, because the love of God has been poured into our hearts by the Holy Spirit which has been given to us. When we were still helpless, at the appointed time, Christ died for the godless. You could hardly find anyone ready to die even for someone upright; though it is just possible that, for a really good person, someone might undertake to die. So it is proof of God's own love for us, that Christ died for us while we were still sinners. How much more can we be sure, therefore, that, now that we have been justified by his death, we shall be saved through him from the retribution of God. For if, while we were enemies, we were reconciled to God through the death of his Son, how much more can we be sure that, being now reconciled, we shall be saved by his life. What is more, we are filled with exultant trust in God, through our Lord Jesus Christ, through whom we have already gained our reconciliation. (Romans 5:1–11)

I take today words from our epistle: 'Since we are justified by faith, we have peace with God through our Lord Jesus Christ.' The words 'justification by faith' have grown to be a watchword or rallying cry of a section of the Church – the evangelicals and the Lutherans amongst others – indicating a special emphasis of the Christian message, 'salvation through faith alone' in contrast to 'salvation through works of the law'. These first words are really a kind of shorthand – well suited by their brevity and used by St Paul – but theologically speaking they are not strictly accurate. For the reality is that we are justified, not by faith, but by the mercy and grace of God, and apart from God's mercy there can be no justification or forgiveness. It is faith which enables us to accept this forgiveness, to appropriate to ourselves God's saving power. Paul has already made it clear in this same epistle, 'justified by his *grace*', he writes, 'as a gift through the redemption which is in Christ Jesus . . . to be *received* by *faith*' (3:24). Or to the people of Ephesus, 'by *grace* you have been saved *through faith*' (Ephesians 2:8).

Faith, then, is that which enables us to lay hold of God's saving grace. We are to see it as God's gift. God is the prime mover in everything, but on our part we are to stir up that gift, exercising it in the challenging circumstances of life. Only so will it grow as a grain of mustard seed and eventually become as a shrub. 'Lord, increase our faith.' 'Lord, I believe, help thou mine unbelief.'

This shortened phrase is not without point because it reminds us of our part in the salvation process. God's part – grace and mercy – will never be lacking, but we shall not experience it if we fail to lay hold of it. When in India I was told of people in the south dying of starvation although they lived close to a lake plentiful with fish. Since they did not belong to the fisherman caste it was unlawful for them to catch fish and so they died in the midst of plenty. So people today die with the bounty of God's mercy all around them because they do not lay hold by faith on what may be truly theirs.

'Justification by faith', to use the shortened phrase, stands in opposition to 'justification by works'. It is a constant temptation to attempt to justify ourselves before God by the works which we perform. Works may indeed reveal the quality of our faith, and their absence reveals, as St James reminds us, that faith is dead, but we are not saved by our works, but by the grace of God through faith. This is the work of God, says Jesus, that you *believe* in him whom God has sent (John 6:29). The person grounded in Christ cannot but reveal their roots in life and action. Works become fruits, spontaneously generated, if the tree be planted in the right soil.

'Justification by faith' may also stand in contrast to 'justification by feelings'. How often may we not be tempted to measure our standing with God by what our feelings seem to be telling us.

But what a fraud feelings are! And yet so often we allow ourselves to be victimised by them. I think that probably the greatest indication of maturity in the Christian life may be measured by the extent to which we allow ourselves to be governed by faith and not by feelings.

One great value of rule, whether of the cloister or in private life, is that it enables us to escape from being victimised by our feelings. Rule enables us to rise above our feelings so that we do not set aside prayer or work when mood or emotion are acting against us. And our rule, of course, is based on faith, faith in what in our calmer and more collected moments we have seen to be right, or it may be what others have seen to be right for us.

And so, says St Paul, being justified by faith we have peace with God through our Lord Jesus Christ. We are to enter into a peace which, through Christ, is already ours, as an heir enters into an inheritance which has already become his own. Once again our feelings are secondary. The ocean seems rough and the waves are high when the wind is strong, but below the surface there is a calm of many fathoms deep. It is not an unfitting picture of the Christian life, often stirred uneasily at surface level, but with a deep and strong reserve of peace, and there will be days when we will be made aware of this, when the calm spreads to the surface, when the feelings of peace break through, suffusing life with a deep contentment and joy. But we are to depend on none of this, and certainly not to be attached to it, as though by right. It cannot always be so. For our sakes and for our growth in the Spirit we may believe it must not always be so. Only faith is the necessity at all times, and if we hold to God in faith we shall be taken through stress and storm into a solid and lasting peace.

～32～

Listening with the Heart

Blessed Lord, who hast caused all holy scriptures to be written for our learning: Grant that we may in such wise hear them, read, mark, learn, and inwardly digest them, that by patience and comfort of thy holy Word, we may embrace and ever hold fast the blessed hope of everlasting life, which thou hast given us in our Saviour Jesus Christ.

Our collect for the second Sunday in Advent calling us to be attentive to the message of scripture was composed in 1549, that is to say during the Reformation period, and it reflects one of the aims of the Reformation, to give to the people an 'Open Bible', to make available to them the word of God in their own language through the hearing and reading of the scriptures. It is not surprising that 'hearing' comes before 'reading' for Tyndale's Bible, the first in English, had been printed only twenty-five years before and could not have been widely available; and even if it had been there would not have been many sufficiently literate to read it for themselves. So for the most part we may believe people came to know the scriptures though hearing them read, either in the Offices of the Church – the eucharist was relatively rare – or when their parish priest visited their homes; or in some households there would have been a member of the family who could read to others. Often, we may suppose, today's collect would precede such readings, calling upon the assembly not merely to hear and read the word of God, but to mark or note carefully what they heard, to learn or store up in their minds passages on which they might draw in their daily lives, and finally to digest, that is to say assimilate, the message, making it a very part of themselves. Apart from this, the rest would be in vain. 'If thou knewest the whole Bible by heart, what would it profit thee without love and saving grace.' The quotation is from *The Imitation of Christ*.

Considerable attention was paid to knowledge of the Bible in the childhood of most of us here [at Bede House], no doubt in the hope that what was lodged in the mind would feed the heart and move the will. It may not have mattered much if this did not happen at once. I suspect we are grateful that at one stage we had to learn what we then little understood but on which we are now able to draw.

I am led to ask what should be the manner of our hearing of the scriptures. And I ask this following a conversation with a sister of a contemplative order who told me that she found the eucharist with its three lessons rather overweighted with Bible reading and that the giving of her mind to these readings was a disturbance in the total act of worship. It seemed to me that she was listening cerebrally as a student might attend to a lecture trying to miss none of the points presented for consideration. The way for her, I suggested, was to compose herself in silent prayer, to put her mind into her heart and sit or stand in the presence of God. She could not but be aware of the words of scripture in the background flowing round her and through her. Meanwhile she, in her interior prayer, was in the most receptive state for the Spirit to reach her (perhaps through the words being read) and act upon her as he would. Not every verse can be relevant for every member of the congregation, and in this state she would be in a position to be receptive to what was applicable to her own needs. If she were to pass through the full readings without remembering what was presented, this would not mean the time would be lost. She would have been sustained in prayer, and the scriptural readings and her presence with others in the action of the eucharist would have helped to that end. We do not need to remember what we ate for breakfast in order that our strength may be maintained. The food nourished us at the time and will go on nourishing us until we eat again.

Naturally, the way I have outlined – this listening with the heart – might not be for all, but I imagine that what I said to this sister must find a response in all of you here. We might say very much the same of the other great portions of scripture which reach us through the psalms of the daily office. Vocal prayer may be truly contemplative, as Father Augustine Baker of *Holy Wisdom* reminds us. And generally speaking, in community this is what we shall find it to be. Father Baker, you may remember, gives three degrees of vocal prayer. In the first degree we attend to and reflect upon the words and the sense of the sentences, turning them over in our minds. In the second degree, suited to those practised in interior prayer (and here I have in mind the sister to whom I was talking), the attention is to God rather than to the words and is far more beneficial than the former. Hence it would be both 'prejudicial and unreasonable' to abandon prayer of this degree for that of the first. 'For since' continues Fr Baker 'all vocal prayer in scripture or otherwise were ordained only to this end, to supply and furnish the soul that needs with good matter by which it may be united to God, a soul that has already attained that end ought not to be separated therefrom.'

And there we might think the matter ended. But not so. Fr Baker gives what he calls 'a third and most sublime degree'. The number called to this, he says, is very small, indeed only those who have come to perfect contemplation, those in whom the imagination is 'so subdued to the Spirit, that it cannot rest upon anything which will distract it'. Perhaps we have sometimes seen flashes of that in others, glimpses of what in the saints may have been an almost continuous state. This is not something which can be achieved, even by grace, nor should we attempt to achieve it. It can only be prepared for by continuing faithfulness in the state to which we are now called and it will come eventually, if it does come, as God's gift to those who are ready to receive it.[1]

1. Both quotations from Father Baker are from *Holy Wisdom*, Third Treatise, Section 1, chapter 2.

∼33∼

Let God Be the Pacemaker

'Lord, if you will, you can make me clean', and Jesus said 'I will, be thou clean'. And immediately his leprosy was cleansed.

(Matthew 8:2–3)

It seems that the leper did not doubt that Jesus could heal him but that he was doubtful whether Jesus wanted to heal him. How often may we not be like that in times of sickness? Is it God's will that I should be healed here and now, or does God have some work to do within me which can only be done if I am laid aside for a while? It is likely that this is a dilemma which belongs to us all. Brother Edward of the Village Evangelists writes to a sick person of these two movements of the soul. I quote:

> There is a constant struggle between the desire not to fail in faith in God's healing and restoring power, and the desire to accept the cross and prove his strength made perfect in weakness. All leads to trust, I find. I think the way out is to keep our eyes on God's glory, and to live for today whatever it holds, and to offer thankfully our present condition whether health or pain.

Leprosy in biblical times was seen as a type of sin; not surprisingly for it corrupted the body as sin defiles the soul, and it isolated people from one another as sin isolates them from God. The Greek word used for cleansing can be used literally in a physical sense or spiritually to denote a cleansing from sin. Everyone who is aware of their spiritual need may come to Jesus with this prayer, 'Lord, if you will you can make me clean', and know that he can have no other will but to complete in us the good work which he has begun.

Yet to be made whole, complete, integrated people can never be, as bodily healing *could* be, the work of a moment, but is the process of a lifetime and even then to be completed on the other side of death. This is the sanctifying work of the Holy Spirit and our part is to co-operate, on the one hand not to be careless or indolent, or failing in faith or courage, and on the other not to be over-eager, impatient, precipitate. The Holy Spirit is the pacemaker. Over-zealous people are those who try to make the pace for him. We can separate ourselves from him just as surely by forging ahead as by lagging behind. One of the hardest lessons for good people of eager and ardent nature to learn is to conquer their weaknesses or imperfections in the Holy Spirit's time and not in their own. The more humiliating the weakness, the more likely is this to be so. And the reason, it is to be feared, is not because we want to gain the victory for the sake of God's glory – though we may deceive ourselves that that is so – but because we cannot bear to look at ourselves and say, 'Lord, that is just like me, and apart from your grace I can do no other'. Yet in this very weakness God's strength is being made perfect until he shall see fit to deliver us from it. The great thing is that we shall always look beyond it in hope of completion being God's ultimate plan for us. St Paul's thorn in the flesh was, we are told, a safeguard against pride, and our own weakness is likely in God's mercy to be that, and hence the wisdom of conquering it in God's time and not in ours.

The following words in a letter from St Francis de Sales, with which I will close, struck me forcibly when I came across them the other day. I have adapted them slightly to reduce their length.

> The remedy is not to struggle, not to make eager attempts to fly, as your wings have not yet grown and you lack power for too great an effort. Be patient. You are too ardent and headstrong, you thirst and long inordinately for good-ness, and you rush forward to meet the object of your desire, but in vain for you do not yet have wings. And this constant flutter exhausts your strength. Of course you must try to fly but do it gently and without struggling and without getting flustered. This straining eagerness is a fault of yours and it comes from a lack of resignation. You do resign yourself but it is with a BUT for you want this and that and you struggle to get it. A simple desire is not contrary to resignation, but a panting heart, fluttering wings, an agi-tated will, and many restless movements – all these

undoubtedly add up to lack of resignation. Courage, my dear Sister; if our *will* belongs to God we are surely his. You have all that is necessary but without feeling it; that is no great loss. Do you know what you ought to do? As your wings have not grown try to find pleasure in not flying.

Thanksgiving

The good news revealed to the simple. The Father and the Son
Just at this time, filled with joy by the Holy Spirit, he said, 'I bless you, Father, Lord of heaven and of earth, for hiding these things from the learned and the clever and revealing them to little children. Yes, Father, for that is what it has pleased you to do. 'Everything has been entrusted to me by my Father: and no one knows who the Son is except the Father, and who the Father is except the Son and those to whom the Son chooses to reveal him.'

The privilege of the disciples
Then turning to his disciples he spoke to them by themselves, 'Blessed are the eyes that see what you see, for I tell you that many prophets and kings wanted to see what you see, and never saw it; to hear what you hear, and never heard it. (Luke 10:21–24).

How moving are these words! 'I thank you, Father, Lord of heaven and earth' (10:21). Thanksgiving is, perhaps, the noblest of the responses to God which it is open to us to make. It is closely linked with praise and adoration. Thanksgiving resembles petition in that it is essentially a person-to-person matter. We have on several occasions had cause to notice that if petition were to drop out of prayer it would not be long before we lost the element of personality within the being of God. Perhaps we should modify that by saying that it is petition and thanksgiving together which keep alive the awareness of those attributes in God which enable us to call him Father.

A life irradiated with thanksgiving is the surest mark of a deeply grounded Christian character. Thanksgiving and humility are closely linked, and necessarily so, for in thanksgiving we acknowledge our dependence upon one another. The grateful person is always being weaned from the independence and isolation which is at the root of pride. It is difficult to see how a person perfected in thanksgiving would not, too, be perfected in humility. The measure of our humility is to be seen in the measure of our thankfulness. 'Be thankful,' says St Paul, 'whatever happens.' It is only as we grow in dependence upon God, knowing by faith that he works for the best through all circumstances, however contrary they may now appear to be, that we can hope to obey the apostle's command.

It is particularly appropriate that we at Bede House should treasure thanksgiving, for our venerable patron was a man pre-eminent in thanksgiving. You will remember how Cuthbert[1] writes of Bede in his sickness:

> Daily he gave us lessons, who were his pupils, and spent the rest of the day in chanting the psalter as best he could. The whole of every night he passed cheerfully in prayer and giving God thanks, except only when brief slumber intervened; and in the same way when he woke up he would at once take up again the familiar melodies of Scripture, not ceasing to spread out his hands in thanksgiving to God. In all truth I can say it: I never saw or heard any man so diligent in returning thanks to the living God. Surely a blessing was upon him.

This seems to have been the habitual manner of Bede's life, a life lived in a round of praise, adoration and thanksgiving. In this the psalter was his chief instrument and instructor. It might perhaps have been said of Bede, as St Antony the Great said of himself: 'I psalmed down the devil'. It is in the power of constant praise that the victory can be gained over fear or anxiety or depression. Paul and Silas psalmed down the devil as they sang hymns and praises through the night in their dungeon prison in circumstances which might have led ordinary people to despair. A praising corporate presence in every prison and hospital of the land would have a healing effect beyond the power of most to imagine.

But to end on a personal note. It is particularly appropriate that my final talk to you should be on the subject of thanksgiving for I have so much to be thankful for, and especially in these last three years through the beauty and blessings of this place, the love and care you have given me, and the many friends I have made. To say more would be embarrassing to all of us, and in any case a grateful heart is more eloquent than many words. I know your blessing rests upon me as I go, and that I shall have your continued prayers for God's strength and guidance in the years ahead. And may God bless you all, and strengthen and uphold you in the special and high vocation he has laid upon you, and make you a blessing to many. 'Have peace in your hearts,' wrote St Seraphim, 'have peace in your hearts, and thousands shall be converted around you.'

1. Cuthbert was a disciple of Bede. He later became abbot of Jarrow.